Virginia
Country

*Inside the Private Historic Homes
of the Old Dominion*

English Colonial 1690–1720

Toddsbury

Set in the Tidewater country of Gloucester County, Toddsbury has been lived in continuously for 300 years, a distinction held by only a few other homes in America.

Built by Thomas Todd on the North River around 1690, Toddsbury was home to four generations of Todds and two generations of Tabbs (Todd descendants). In a letter dated 1847, sent from a guest at nearby Auburn to his family back home in New England, the correspondent describes the location of twenty-six plantations in the area belonging to "respectable families," where "every one keeps a carriage and horses and visiting is kept up every day of the year." The writer further notes that more than half of the proprietors of these plantations are related to a Dr. Tabb (his host) and a "most friendly intercourse exists between all of them." The Tabbs of Toddsbury were among this group. Today, the residents of Gloucester and Matthews Counties still travel up and down the rivers to visit each other's homes, and many of these Tidewater neighbors are related.

Toddsbury was sold out of the family in 1880 to John Mott. The current owner, Breck Montague, is engaged to Mary Williams, a Mott descendant, whose mother grew up at Toddsbury.

Driving down Toddsbury's lane, lined first with woods and then opening into an alley lined with large, old maple trees, the visitor is rewarded at last by the white brick, gambrel-roofed house. To the left is a one-acre square, brick-walled garden. Behind the house and to its right is the North River. Standing on a rounded point in the river, Toddsbury affords water views to the east and south.

These river views are enhanced by a collection of eighteenth, nineteenth and twentieth

Right: The east parlor windows boast detailed paneling around recessed frames, as well as beautiful views of the North River.

century outbuildings, including stables, a freestanding kitchen, and a dairy. The oldest is a round ice house located by the entrance lane. Next to the garden is the Todd family graveyard.

In the small, brick entry hall on the north side of the house, visitors are greeted by a row of pegs with jackets and hats hanging. To the south of the entry hall is a central stair hall which opens onto a porch facing south to the river.

Off the central hall to the east is a fully panelled parlor, with windows recessed in arches on each side of the chimney breast. In place of windows on each side of the chimney breast, the west parlor has small closets with doors. Located across the central hall, the west parlor has painted blue paneling and numerous portraits and beautifully crafted period furniture. On a windowpane of handblown glass someone scratched an illegible name and dated it 17[?]. This room is clearly eighteenth century in appearance, and imparts a sense of what Toddsbury was like nearly 300 years ago.

The dining room, located in the north part of the ell, is filled with family treasures, including a beautiful dining table, sideboard and antique silver. Off the dining room is the north hall and back stairs. On the landing of the stairs are miniature samples of furniture used by cabinetmakers in the eighteenth century.

In the middle of the house is the nearly square central hall, to which Montague has added bookcases to three of the walls. A spinet piano is against the wall below the stairs. Montague says he and his children use this room often, and spend many hours there reading and listening to music.

Left: A view of the house from the walled garden shows its gambrel roof, a style that was common at the end of the seventeenth century.

Above: Cheery sunflowers border the small kitchen garden.

Standing on a rounded point
in the North River,
Toddsbury affords water
views to the east and south.

Above: A central passageway in the barn was designed to allow carriages and riders to pass through with ease.

Right: Like all of the main rooms at Toddsbury, the dining room is richly paneled.

Montague's favorite room is the screened, wooden porch, added sometime in the eighteenth century. It has an enclosed room above it on the second floor. "The porch takes advantage of the breezes, great light and a view of the river to the south," says Montague. Not a proponent of air conditioning, Montague relies on those river breezes to cool the house during the hot and humid Tidewater summers.

Toddsbury is at once breathtakingly elegant, yet warm and inviting. Each room offers a beautiful setting for Montague's collections of photos, paintings, books, and family memorabilia. "It is the feeling as much as the age [of Toddsbury] that appeals to me," Montague says.

Breck Montague feels a keen sense of family history at Toddsbury. He inherited the home from his late aunt, the noted preservationist Gay Montague Moore. The Montague family's tenure at Toddsbury dates back only to the middle of this century, but their arrival in Virginia goes back to 1621, when their ancestor Peter Montague arrived from Buckinghamshire, England. Breck Montague's grandfather, Andrew Jackson Montague, was governor of Virginia from 1902 to 1906.

Today, Breck Montague takes a hands-on approach to preservation at Toddsbury. "I pay attention to detail and I try to fix things myself," he says.

That appreciation for small things goes beyond the physical for Montague, who says he especially relishes "the smell, the quiet, the nature" of Toddsbury. "When I turn down the lane on my way home, I turn my car radio off and roll down my window," says Montague. "I smell the humus of the forest, and I feel the peace and tranquility of the whole place."

Left: Family portraits line the stairs of the central hall, which doubles as a music room and parlor.

Above right: The blue room, or west parlor, is filled with family pieces and antiques collected by the owner's late aunt, noted preservationist Gay Montague Moore.

Below right: Virginia's Tidewater rivers served as roads during colonial times and provide leisure for local residents today.

Tuckahoe

Located west of Richmond on the James River, Tuckahoe is one of only a few American plantation houses that has survived nearly unaltered. Students of history know that Tuckahoe was the boyhood home of Thomas Jefferson, but what they may not know is that the main house and the plantation road with its outbuildings and dependencies are among the most complete eighteenth-century complexes in North America.

The sense of history and family at Tuckahoe is palpable. The beautifully preserved house holds its original woodwork, windows, and flooring, along with period furniture. Yet every room of the house is used by the owners, Addison "Tad" and Sue Thompson, and their four children.

Built by Thomas Randolph between 1714 and 1720, Tuckahoe was one of many Randolph family estates, this one named for *tockawaugh*, the Native American name for

Above: Tuckahoe's unusual H-shape, seen from the west side of the house, includes the 1712 wing on the left and the new center and right wings, built in 1730.

Below: In 1780, Colonel Ball scratched his name in the glass of a dining room window, and Mariah Horsemanden Byrd of Westover added her mark to another pane in 1842.

Students of history
know that Tuckahoe
was the boyhood home
of Thomas Jefferson.

a lily that flourished along the streams of the plantation. Thomas's father, William Randolph of Turkey Island (on the lower James River), emigrated from England around 1673. Like Robert "King" Carter (see Sabine Hall, page 102), Randolph prospered and was able to establish each of his seven sons on his own plantation, Thomas at Tuckahoe and his brothers nearby. He also purchased the land for Cool Water for his daughter (see page 46).

Tuckahoe sits on a high bluff on the north bank of the James River. Between the house and the river is a wide flood plain that contains an unusual canal dug perpendicular to the river, with a circular turning pool at the end. This allowed goods to be brought upriver to Tuckahoe and easily unloaded at the end of the canal.

In colonial times, Tuckahoe was a thriving plantation. There were at least a dozen plantation outbuildings to the west of the house along the plantation road. Still standing today are three slave cabins, the old stable, a smokehouse, storehouse, office, and kitchen. To the east of the house is the original schoolhouse.

It is in this schoolhouse that Thomas Jefferson began his education. Jefferson's father, Peter, had moved his family to Tuckahoe in 1745 upon the death of Thomas Randolph's son, William. William Randolph was the first cousin of Peter Jefferson's wife, Jane, and Peter was guardian of William's son, Thomas Mann Randolph. The Jeffersons lived at Tuckahoe for seven years, until 1752, while Peter Jefferson oversaw the plantation. Thomas Mann Randolph and Thomas Jefferson were just two years apart in age and became lifelong friends.

After the Jeffersons moved back to Shadwell in Albemarle County, the Randolphs continued to live at

Above left: A bedroom believed to have been a young Thomas Jefferson's holds a Jefferson-era brass bedwarmer (next to the fireplace) and an eighteenth-century camp bed used on military expeditions (on the left).

Left: The "plantation street" at Tuckahoe, shown with the old smokehouse in the foreground.

Right: The celebrated frieze in Tuckahoe's north stair hall provides the only example of this type of carving in Virginia.

Tuckahoe until they sold it out of the family in 1830. The plantation house and surrounding 560 acres passed through a succession of owners until Tad Thompson's grandparents, Isabelle Ball Baker and N. Addison Baker, bought the property.

Thomas Randolph relied heavily on English architecture of the period in the design of Tuckahoe. An H-shaped house, Tuckahoe has two main wings, each with a center hall dividing two rooms. The wings are connected by a large central salon. Throughout the house, the rooms are paneled in walnut and pine.

Each of the two main wings has a staircase. The newel post of the north stair is a classic Corinthian column ornamented with carved vines and flowers, the stair brackets are carved with acanthus and five-petaled blossoms, and the landing and gallery fascias are carved with flowing flowers and leaves. The south stair is much simpler, with the rail and newel carved in a spiral pattern to match the balusters.

To the west of the north stairs is the west or "white" parlor, named for its white painted paneling. Across the hall is the elegant east parlor where the fireplace is flanked by Corinthian pilasters and arched paneled cupboards.

The central salon functions as a hall to the south wing and as a large reception room. The unpainted paneling in the salon was probably patterned on the designs made popular in Moxon's *Mechanick Exercises*, published in London in 1703. The south wing also contains two finely paneled rooms, the dining room to the west and the family parlor to the east.

Today, a long cedar-lined lane leads to Tuckahoe and ends in a T-intersection facing the front lawn and house to the south. To the west is the plantation road and to the east is a lane that goes to the stables, tenant houses, and a cabinetmaker's shop. Tuckahoe still functions much as it did in colonial times. The plantation staff lives in the tenant houses and former plantation cabins. Tad Thompson maintains an office in the building that housed the original plantation office, and a cabinetmaker uses the shop to produce beautiful cabinetry for Tuckahoe and other clients.

It is easy to forget that an energetic family of six lives in the house, yet the soccer and carpool schedules posted on the narrow stairs leading to the English basement in the south wing tell us this is the 1990s, not the 1790s. The English basement is the only area in Tuckahoe that has been significantly changed. A large, modern kitchen and family room have been created in what was once a dark and uninviting space.

The plantation staff often gathers in the kitchen for morning coffee and to catch up on Tuckahoe news. It is common to see customers of the cabinetmaker driving down the lane or horseback riders heading to and from Tuckahoe's stables. ❧

Above: In the dining room, a portrait of the current owner hangs over a bow-front Sheraton sideboard, and in the corner stands an American sugar chest with a pewter cover.

Left: The old brick kitchen probably replaced the original frame structure around 1780.

Left: Built-in cupboards in the "burnt room" house family china.

Above: Delicate flowers contrast with the rough surfaces of the handmade bricks used to build Tuckahoe's old kitchen.

Right: A plaque commemorates Thomas Jefferson's school days at Tuckahoe.

Upper Weyanoke

Above: Paths meander next to the James River, which at Upper Weyanoke is a few miles wide.

For 100 years after English colonists first settled Jamestown in 1607, life along the James River was plagued by a series of battles between Native Americans and settlers. Determined to establish themselves in this new land, leaders of the Virginia Company of London, and later of the newly-formed colonial government, built garrisons along the river to protect themselves from Indian attacks.

In the early 1600s, land along the north bank of the James River in what is today Charles City County, was inhabited by the Weyanoke Indians, one of the largest groups of the Powhatan chiefdom. The Weyanoke Indians, who originally lived on a peninsula along the James River, were lead in those days by a woman, who went by the sole name of "Queen of the Weyanokes." Weyanoke means "land of sassafras," and this native variety of trees is still common in the area.

Around 1620, Opechancanough, brother of Chief Powhatan, gave approximately 2,000 acres

of land to Sir George Yeardley. Sometime after the English-Powhatan War of 1622, during which 300 colonists were killed, a small brick garrison house was built near the banks of the river. Today, that brick cottage is part of an estate called Upper Weyanoke.

A few years later, Governor Yeardley sold Upper Weyanoke to Abraham Peirsey, who in turn sold it to William Harwood in 1644. The Harwoods remained at Upper Weyanoke for several generations.

In 1850, a Harwood descendant, Fielding Lewis Douthat, brought his bride, Mary Willis Marshall, granddaughter of U.S. Chief Justice John Marshall, to live at Upper Weyanoke. The Douthats lived in a second house that had been built on the property in the mid-nineteenth century. In the 1940s, Mr. and Mrs. Henry Bahnsen bought the property. The large house was abandoned (and remains so today) and the garrison cottage served as the main residence.

What the Bahnsens found at Upper Weyanoke was a simple, one-and-a-half-story house with foot-thick walls laid in Flemish-bond brick. Possibly the oldest house on the James River (although this has never been confirmed), Upper Weyanoke has the original fireplace in the English basement and wooden floors with hand-wrought nails. Two plain, rectangular rooms make up the first floor of the original portion of the house, and an enclosed staircase leads to two small bedrooms upstairs. The Bahnsens significantly expanded the little house to include a glass sun porch on the south end and a one-story north wing connected by a hyphen-shaped nook.

As strong and lasting as the original house has been, it was in peril of being lost just a few years ago. Over the centuries, the north shoreline of the James River has shifted dramatically and the garrison house, literally hanging out over the jagged shoreline, was just inches from dropping into the river. After much effort and expense, 170 truckloads of earth and riprap for the foundations were deposited along the shoreline. The

Left: The parlor walls are thick and the window somewhat small, features that remind visitors of the martial origins of this former garrison.

23

No one knows how many garrison houses may have been built along the James River after the 1622 massacre, however, Upper Weyanoke is the only one that remains.

Left: Roses drape the windows of the modern sun porch.

Above: Many of the doors operate by means of wooden latch and lock systems, hardware restored or created from seventeenth century designs.

Right: An Audubon print hangs over the west parlor in the oldest section of Upper Weyanoke.

current owner, Mrs. John Moon, the Bahnsen's daughter, is confident that the river bank has been preserved forever.

Preservation and excavation are very much a part of life at Upper Weyanoke. Several archaeological digs have unearthed numerous pipe stems and arrow heads on the property. No one knows how many garrison houses may have been built along the James River after the 1622 massacre, however, Upper Weyanoke is the only one that remains. A previous resident, Miss Eleanor Douthat, who was born at Upper Weyanoke, told Mrs. Moon about the foundations of what was probably another garrison house near the house. Her tip has led some to believe that two or more garrisons were originally on the site at Upper Weyanoke.

Garden paths between the garrison house and the large house are lined with boxwood hedges that are 250 years old and more than thirty-five feet high. The paths were laid out along the river by Mary Marshall Douthat around the mid-1800s, and contain original fig bushes, old crape myrtles, and beautiful magnolia trees.

The Bahnsens bought Upper Weyanoke as a country retreat and a place for Mr. Bahnsen to fix things, says Mrs. Moon. Bahnsen found plenty to fix, but Upper Weyanoke has also become a place for four generations of the Bahnsen family to relax. The large window in the new north wing has two pairs of binoculars ready for spotting bald eagles along this nearly mile-wide stretch of the James River. What started as a fortress more than 300 years ago has become a family retreat—a place where the slow movement of the river mirrors the lives of the owners. ❧

Above left: Ribbons of every color attest to the championship qualities of the Bahnsen's show dogs.

Below left: Sprightly coneflowers are among the myriad perennials in Upper Weyanoke's gardens.

Right: Upper Weyanoke stands but a few yards from the James River. In the 1600s, it may have been one of two garrison houses strategically located here.

Colonial 1720–1790

Blandfield

Their search for a bit of Rappahannock River shoreline on which to establish a duck blind led the late James C. Wheat, Jr., and his wife, Wylie, to a greater find: Blandfield, a splendid mid-Georgian home set on 3,500 acres. Built by prominent colonial planter Robert Beverley in 1770 on land first patented by Major Robert Beverley around 1660, Blandfield was a showcase for Beverley and his new wife, Maria Byrd Carter of nearby Sabine Hall (see page 102). The house became the topic of many of Beverley's writings, from letters to diaries detailing the paint colors and building materials he had specially ordered for his grand home. As is apparent, the details were well worth the effort and expense.

In his letter book on November 18, 1763, Beverley made it clear he was happy at Blandfield: "I assure you I am vastly in my Domestick way of life. . . and unless some accident should disturb my Repose, I shall Not alter my Method of Life."

Blandfield remained in the Beverley family for nearly 300 years before it came on the market in 1983. In a state of disrepair, it was earmarked for development by real estate speculators, but the Wheat family interceded, purchasing the house and grounds and commencing with the restoration of its three floors, attached wings, and out-buildings. The task could have been complicated by the fact that Mr. Wheat was blind, but the successful Richmond financier had never allowed his handicap to daunt him before. "We had thought we would retire and restore an old mill in the mountains near Lexington [Virginia]," said Wylie Wheat, "but that was all changed for us by Blandfield."

Armed with the extensive writings of Robert Beverley and the modern interpretations of

Right: A pastel portrait of William Henry Bagwell Custis hangs over the Hepplewhite sideboard in the dining room.

Although the Wheat's twentieth-century
way of life differs from that of the founder,
they share Beverley's love for Blandfield.

architects Edward Chappell and Alan Morledge of Colonial Williamsburg, the Wheats undertook one of the most extensive restorations ever of a private home in America. Thirteen years later, this restoration continues.

The main house is a visual delight. With stunning color, the Wheats have made Blandfield's public rooms on the first floor historically accurate without making them feel or look like museum tableaux. No stairs are visible in the great hall in the front of the house. Instead, two staircases rise in another hall that runs the width of the house and divides the front three rooms from the back three. Directly behind the great hall is a large parlor that opens to a back porch, added in the nineteenth century, with a spectacular view across the lawn to the Rappahannock River.

In the north and south corners at the rear of the house are charming parlors. Off the great hall to the south is a guest bedroom that, during Robert Beverley's day, was the family dining room. Today, the dining room is located to the west of the great hall and contains beautiful family and period furniture. Again, a wide hall upstairs runs the width of the house, an unusual feature in the eighteenth century, dividing the six bedrooms into three in front and three in back.

In the course of their restoration efforts, the Wheats learned that the Blandfield they had purchased was dramatically different from Beverley's original. Research conducted by Vanessa Patrick, of Colonial Williamsburg, showed that

Left: Blandfield's lawns afford a view of the pond and the Rappahannock River beyond.

Above right: Custom-made bed draperies festoon the downstairs guest room.

Below right: A portrait of the Honorable John Spencer, grandfather of the Duchess of Devonshire, hangs over the hall mantel.

Overleaf: Blandfield's Palladian design was greatly influenced by English houses of the same period.

sometime around 1840, intricate interior paneling and molding was replaced with plain woodwork, and each of the two original staircases, complete with balusters and rails, was replaced with nineteenth-century versions. These and other details have been lovingly restored by the Wheats. They created new milled woodwork, including overmantels, door surrounds, wainscotting, and moldings for each room, and they replicated the marble fireplace surrounds from stone quarried in King of Prussia, Pennsylvania.

Mrs. Wheat again credits the staff at Colonial Williamsburg Foundation for their guidance with the interior decoration. "Margaret Pritchard and Ronald Hurst have helped immensely in the selection of paint, wallpaper, and prints." Wallpapers were hung using eighteenth-century techniques. Squares of paper were applied to the walls and then painted with solid, often vivid, colors, resulting in rich textures and color variations. The restorers also used printed wallpapers, including a pattern in the front hall called Pillars and Galleries, found during restoration research in the Library of Congress and copied for Blandfield, and a brilliant yellow-on-yellow documentary wallpaper in the south parlor that was copied from a pattern in Colonial Williamsburg and handprinted in England.

The Wheats chose furniture scaled to fit the proportions of the public rooms, with their fourteen-foot ceilings. Upstairs and down they have interspersed Wheat family furnishings, including period English and Welsh antiques, English mirrors, antique maps, and family crests. An impressive collection of Catesby ornithology prints is hung in the north parlor.

Although the Wheat's twentieth-century way of life differs from that of the founder, they share Beverley's love for Blandfield. The late Mr. Wheat often enjoyed being with his friends while they hunted on the property. Today, Wheat's son James C. Wheat III and his family and friends still hunt duck, wild turkey, and dove, and fish in the river, located one-and-a-half miles below the house.

Mrs. Wheat and her son have frequent houseguests, and it is not unusual for visiting dignitaries, historians, or Beverley family descendants to drop by for a tour.

During the initial phase of Blandfield's restoration, James Wheat spent much of his time corresponding with architects, historians, and preservationists, and often conducted house tours for friends and family. Although unable to see the architectural details of his house, his amazing memory enabled him to give accurate and detailed descriptions of his beloved home. Since his death in 1993, Wylie Wheat has carried on the restoration work. With the ongoing help of preservationists and historians, she directs the day-to-day decision making. There are paint colors to choose, drapes to design, boxwoods to replant—her chores are legion.

In all her tasks, Wylie Wheat is ever mindful of the details described by Robert Beverley and embraced by her husband when restoration began nearly fifteen years ago. The spirits of these Blandfield men live on in the great house, and their presence is in the glorious details that distinguish this Georgian masterpiece from other of the world's grand homes. ⋗

Right: The design of the painted floorcloth in the dining room is based on a 1730s model.

Brandon

In 1616, the Earls of Pembroke and Southampton, Sir Francis Bacon and Captain John Smith, among others, signed a land patent granting John Martin 7,000 acres of land along the James River in the new colony of Virginia. Martin called this huge plantation Brandon, his wife's family name. A survivor of the first Jamestown settlement fifteen miles downriver, Martin used the James as the route to his land. He began growing tobacco and other crops on what is today, the oldest continuous agricultural operation in America.

Martin sold Brandon in 1637 to John Sadler, Richard Quiney, and William Barber, whose heirs continued to farm Brandon until 1720, when they sold the plantation to Nathaniel Harrison. Harrison never moved to Brandon, but instead lived at the plantation of his wife's family in Stafford County.

In 1765, Harrison's son Nathaniel II married and moved to Brandon. The younger Harrison's good friend, Thomas Jefferson, served as a groomsman in the wedding. Harrison family tradition holds that Jefferson helped his friend design the house at Brandon. This belief may be due to the obvious influence of elements from Robert Morris's *Select Architecture*, a book published in 1757 and known to have been a source for Thomas Jefferson.

Brandon's unique architecture evolved over a number of years. Nathaniel Harrison II built the center structure and converted two existing one-and-one-half-story houses into two-story wings

Left: Brandon's arched screen and stairs were probably added around 1800.

Overleaf: The 210-foot façade is broken up by large and small sections in the architecture, lending the grand-sized house an intimate and human scale.

that are joined by one-story connections to the center structure. The resulting Palladian-style house has a varied roofline and a 210-foot-long symmetrical façade. Most of the house (with the exception of the two end wings) is one room deep, a common design in Tidewater Virginia because it allows for cross ventilation from river breezes.

The James River has always been important at Brandon. Once, the river was a highway, connecting the plantation to the rest of the world. Now it offers sanctuary for wildlife, and beautiful views for Brandon's current owners, Mr. and Mrs. Robert W. Daniel, Jr. The river also provides rich nutrients to the soil of the 1,600 acres currently farmed at Brandon.

The enormous red-brick barns along the approach to Brandon reveal the importance of farming in the daily lives of the current owners and tenants. The informal park on the land side of the house and the extensive formal gardens on the river side remind us of Brandon's colonial origins. The oldest or terminal wings of the house are laid in a Flemish bond pattern with glazed headers above an English bond water table, a remnant from when the wings were one-and-a-half stories.

The large (twenty seven-by-thirty-foot) center hall of the house is impressive with its triple arch Ionic screen and side staircase. This hall is an arrangement created in the early nineteenth century and not part of the original structure. Flanking the hall are the formal drawing room to the north and the dining room to the south, which are both fully paneled and have pedimented overmantels. However, much of the paneling in the drawing room was replaced after being damaged during the Civil War.

On the south wall of the dining room, steps lead down into a hyphen-shaped nook that today serves as the breakfast room. At the end of the breakfast room in the terminal wing is a hunting room where Mr. Daniel cleans his guns and displays hunting trophies. Across the hall from the hunting room is a parlor that Mrs. Daniel uses to greet guests and store some of her riding clothes.

At the opposite end of the house is another hyphen containing the library. Also in this north terminal wing are two guest bedrooms. Upstairs, Brandon has three separate sections. The main staircase leads to the master bedroom in the center section of the house, and in each terminal wing are stairs leading to guest rooms upstairs. These separated sections impart a feeling of smaller houses within the larger house. The basement runs the entire 210-foot length of the house and gives visitors a true sense of the enormousness of Brandon.

Left: The eighteenth-century four pedestal Hepplewhite dining table is set with china that was a gift to the Daniel family. On the mantel are porcelain jars that once belonged to Marie Antoinette, and the eighteenth-century French screen is hand painted.

Above: The gun room is used for cleaning firearms and displaying hunting trophies.

Harrison family
tradition holds that
Thomas Jefferson
helped design the
house at Brandon.

Above: The formal gardens sweep down the bank to the James River.

Right: The drawing room is elaborately paneled and filled with family pieces. Above the mantel is a Thomas Sully portrait of Peyton Randolph, president of the First Continental Congress.

Far right: On the 1840s secretary in the drawing room is hung a framed list of all the desk's owners.

On every table and shelf are photos of the Daniel family at work and play. Robert Daniel's parents bought Brandon from the Harrisons in 1926 and the younger Daniel has spent his entire life at Brandon. He represented Virginia's 4th District in Congress from 1973 to 1983, and later served as the director of intelligence for the U.S. Department of Energy.

When the Daniels bought the house, the acreage had dwindled from 7,000 to 1,300 acres. During the past seventy years, the Daniel family has lovingly restored the house and much of the farm to its original glory. Today, Brandon has a total of 4,500 acres, supporting crop production of corn, soybeans, wheat, and barley, as well as pasture, woods, and marshes. Mrs. Daniel is an avid equestrian and keeps several horses at Brandon for fox hunting, while Mr. Daniel manages the farm and oversees a large herd of registered Simmental cattle and a hog operation that produces 3,000 pigs annually.

Brandon has seen adversity and change during its 375-year history. The riverside portico bears the scars of two wars. A British ship in the Revolution fired on the house from the river, but did no great damage. During the Civil War, the house was fired upon and later occupied by Union soldiers, who tore out the paneling in the drawing room and used it for firewood. But the carved pineapple on the roof, the symbol of hospitality, has remained, much like the spirit of Brandon, unmarred for three centuries. ❧

Cool Water

More than thirty years ago, Frank Hargrove was flying his Cessna 310 plane over the Virginia countryside, when he spied an old house on the crest of a hill. The house intrigued Hargrove, so he decided to learn more about the place. The house was Cool Water, a mid-eighteenth-century brick farmhouse located in Hanover County next to Cool Water Branch, a creek that flows into the nearby Newfound River.

A Hanover County native and successful insurance executive, Hargrove had never heard of Cool Water, but after purchasing the house in 1966, he set about learning its history. Built by John Price in 1735 for his bride, Mary Randolph, Cool Water was located on approximately 1,500 acres of land purchased for the couple by Mary's father, William Randolph of Turkey Island. John Price was a master carpenter and his skilled work is evident in what was otherwise a basic two-room-over-two-room house with an English basement.

The Price family remained at Cool Water for nearly 150 years. In the 1870s, the house was sold to an Englishwoman, who turned it into a boarding school for girls. The Grubb family bought the house in the 1880s and lived at Cool Water until the 1930s. The next owner was Charles Hall, who bought the house at the Depression price of $2,700 in the 1930s.

By the mid-1960s, when Hargrove discovered it, the house was in bleak shape, but he appreciated its many unique features. Among those features is the interesting and somewhat quirky entrance. Rather than one entrance door, there are two. Approaching from the south, a guest is greeted by two identical front doors each opening directly into one of the original and adjacent first floor

Right: A 1780s walnut corner cupboard made in Virginia's Shenendoah Valley stands in the parlor.

Built in 1735
by master carpenter
John Price for his bride,
Mary Randolph,
Cool Water is located in
Hanover County next
to Cool Water Branch,
a tributary of the
Newfound River.

Left: An authentic Kentucky rifle hangs over the mantel in the old kitchen that now serves as a den.

Above: The unusual double front doors were designed to allow access into the two separate front rooms without creating unnecessary drafts from the outside.

rooms. The room to the east once contained a simple staircase to the second floor, but now it is the master bedroom. The west room is the main parlor and was once connected to the east room by an inside door. The Hargroves believe the two front doors were designed to allow entrance into one room at a time, thus keeping down cold drafts into the other room in this house with no foyer.

Bricked in a flemish bond pattern, Cool Water's main structure is two stories, with one-story, shed-roofed wings at each end. These wings have small, hall-like rooms behind each fireplace in the English basement and on the first floor. Around 1790, a two-story wing was added to the north side of the house with another entrance on the east side of the house. The two sections of the house are divided by a hallway that runs east to west and contains a new set of stairs.

During their 1966 restoration, the Hargroves added a two-story tower on the west side of the house to allow for bathrooms on each floor. The Hargrove's dining room is located in the English basement next to the room that was the original kitchen. The old kitchen now serves as a small study and the remainder of the basement has been remodeled into a charming, modern kitchen. In the small room located behind the first floor parlor fireplace, Hargrove keeps many of his books and several model airplanes.

An enthusiastic pilot, Hargrove has installed a small landing strip on the property. Painted on his simple hangar are the words "Cool Water, Elevation 250." Hargrove keeps a couple of old planes, including a 1947 Taylor Craft. He often meets with other Taylor Craft owners and even holds fly-ins at Cool Water.

When not flying or pursuing other pastimes, Hargrove is busy with his duties as a member of the Virginia House of Delegates. A delegate for sixteen years, Hargrove represents essentially the same district that Patrick Henry represented in the House of Burgesses from 1769 to 1774. While living a few miles southwest of Cool Water at Scotchtown, Henry was elected Virginia's first governor in 1775.

Left: The cozy office behind the parlor fireplace is filled with mementos of Frank Hargrove's many interests.

Right: A modern well house complements Cool Water's 1730s facade.

Coincidentally, the Prices of Cool Water and the Henrys of Scotchtown were neighbors and friends. Mary Randolph Price was the sister of Elizabeth Chiswell, who lived with her husband, John Chiswell, at Scotchtown before Henry bought the house in 1771. A path made by slaves connecting the two plantations still runs through the woods between Cool Water and Scotchtown.

Hargrove and his wife, Oriana, spend much of their time entertaining family and friends at Cool Water, just as the original owners must have done. The Hargroves raised their four children at Cool Water and the house now serves as the site of many family gatherings. Every Thanksgiving, the Hargroves host relatives from as far away as California. Everyone competes for the Cool Water Cup—a clay pigeon shooting contest that brings out the competitive spirit in the family.

Hargrove describes Cool Water as a place where his family has found freedom and tranquility. The Hargrove children grew up riding horses and ponies on the farm, and Oriana Hargrove planted beautiful gardens. "Cool Water is a happy place," says Hargrove, "poor people have lived here and not so poor people—but as far as I can tell, it has always been a happy place." ⚘

Above: The shady gardens and terrace to the north of the house afford beautiful views of the rolling hills beyond.

Right: A silver service on the tea table was purchased by Mrs. Hargrove in Guildford, England, before her marriage. On the far wall is an eighteenth-century English secretary.

Elmwood

Through wars, neglect, and the ravages of centuries, Elmwood has sat prominently and stoically atop a steep ridge on the south side of the Rappahannock River valley in Essex County.

Built around 1770 by Muscoe Garnett, Elmwood is an imposing sight, a brick plantation home with a massive 100-foot façade. The strength of its façade is reinforced in its details, where a closer look reveals brick walls laid in a Flemish bond pattern and a molded water table banding the entire foundation. With a hipped roof and a projecting pavilion displaying a Palladian window above the front door, this elegant, two-story house was a fitting home for Garnett, a Virginian prominent in local politics and society.

James Mercer Garnett received Elmwood as a gift from his father in 1793 upon his marriage to Mary Eleanor Dick Mercer, a first cousin. James Mercer Garnett was, like his father, a respected member of the community and a local politician. He served two terms in the state legislature, two terms in Congress, and was a member of the grand jury that indicted Aaron Burr for treason. Upon his retirement from Congress, Garnett devoted much of his time and energy to the improvement of agriculture and wrote several pamphlets on the subject from his study at Elmwood.

Upon James Mercer Garnett's death, Elmwood passed to his grandson Muscoe Russell Hunter Garnett, son of the deceased James Mercer Garnett, Jr. Breaking with the family tradition of marrying fellow Virginians, Muscoe wed Mary Picton Stevens,

Above right: The upstairs hall doubles as a parlor and library.

Below right: Graves from the 1700s to the 1990s in the private cemetery at Elmwood attest to the house's continuous family habitation.

daughter of the businessman and inventor Edwin Augustus Stevens of Castle Point, Hoboken, New Jersey. By 1861, Muscoe was living with his young bride in the family home. Yankee bride notwithstanding, Muscoe became involved in the war effort, serving in the Confederate House of Representatives. In 1864, he died of typhoid fever, leaving Mary alone at Elmwood with their two small children and the Civil War still raging.

Alarmed at his daughter's predicament, Edwin Stevens arranged with President Lincoln to have a Union gunboat in the command of Mary's cousin Captain Albert Tod proceed up the Rappahannock River and anchor off the estate. Mary at first refused to go with her cousin when he arrived at Elmwood during the cover of night, but the next morning, she acquiesced, returning with her children to New Jersey, where she stayed for the duration of the war.

Mary returned to Elmwood after 1865 and, in 1869, married Edward Parke Custis Lewis, a relative of George Washington. After Mary's death in 1903, Elmwood stood empty for a number of years. The house passed to Mary's son, James Mercer Garnett, and eventually to his sister Mary Barton Picton

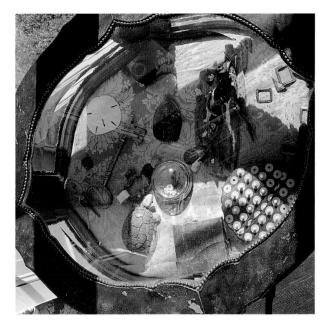

Left: Elmwood's exterior bears classic mid-Georgian details.

Above: A glass-topped table shows off a collection of treasures both old and new.

57

Garnett Mitchell. In 1943, Mrs. Mitchell gave Elmwood to her nephew Muscoe R. H. Garnett, the father of the current owner, Muscoe R. H. Garnett, Jr.

By the 1940s when the elder Muscoe R. H. Garnett inherited Elmwood, the house was in serious disrepair. Mid-nineteenth century porches were falling off the front and back of the Georgian house, plaster was coming off the walls, and the finish was worn off the floors. Garnett and his wife, Helene, undertook a restoration that took more than twenty years to complete, removing derelict and superfluous additions and rebuilding and renovating original elements. By the 1960s, Elmwood once more resembled its 1770 form, outside and in. Victorian porches and a tower were removed, the boxwood garden behind the house was restored, and the inside rooms once again were furnished in eighteenth-century heirlooms.

Elmwood has many classic Tidewater features in its architecture and floor plan, including a large central hall that doubles as a drawing room. The house also boasts elaborate moldings and woodwork. Just inside the front door, the hall forms a T-shape with a recessed stairhall to the east and a matching hall to the west that now contains an elevator. Behind the east stairhall (off the central hall) is the library, which contains original woodwork and a portrait over the mantel of James Mercer Garnett. Across the central hall, to the west, is the sitting room—the only room at Elmwood with its original mantel.

Throughout the house are numerous examples of superb craftsmanship—probably the work of William Buckland, who is believed to have done the woodcarving at Elmwood. The central hall cornice carries a full Doric entablature, and the elliptical arches between the central hall and recessed halls are supported by fluted pilasters. At the far west end of the house is the twenty-by-thirty foot ballroom. The walls have been painted only twice in this elaborate room, first when the house was built and a second time in 1851.

The new owners, Muscoe R. H. Garnett, Jr., and his wife, Roberta, are the seventh generation of Garnetts to live at Elmwood. For the past seventeen years, Muscoe and Roberta have been living in a restored eighteenth-century barn on the property. Muscoe's mother, Helene, passed away earlier this year, leaving this younger generation of Garnetts to settle into Elmwood and carry on the family's tradition of stewardship.

Some things will not change at Elmwood. Roberta will continue to tend horses on the property and Muscoe will still oversee the farm operations. When their two grown children come to Elmwood to visit, the eighth generation of Garnetts will be at home. ⚜

Right: The large front hall serves as a reception area and parlor. The ceiling cornice carries a full Doric entablature.

Left: The ballroom at Elmwood has served as the site of many grand occasions.

Above top: Dogwoods line the back pasture fence at Elmwood.

Above: James Mercer Garnett's portrait is tucked neatly in a Federal overmantel.

Right: From this sunny upstairs bedroom are grand views of the formal gardens.

Eyre Hall

Standing like a white ship becalmed on a sea of grass, Eyre Hall is a house of unparalleled beauty and serenity. The frame structure is built in the typical Eastern Shore architectural style: big house, little house, colonnade, and kitchen, all connected to form a long building with a stair-stepped roofline. But this classic exterior is the only typical element of Eyre Hall.

Located near the banks of Cherrystone Creek, a tidal creek that empties into the Chesapeake Bay north of the town of Cape Charles, Eyre Hall is a testament to the unerring taste and style of the Eyre family.

Littleton Eyre built Eyre Hall on land patented to his grandfather and great-uncles by Governor Berkeley in 1662. The land was repayment for services rendered to King James II by their father, Thomas Eyre. In 1773, Littleton's son Severn inherited the house and surrounding land. Severn Eyre served in the Virginia House of Burgesses from 1766 to 1773. His son John, who next inherited Eyre Hall, is credited with laying out the formal gardens behind the house in 1790.

Built originally as a simple, south-facing, story-and-a-half structure by Littleton Eyre around 1730, Eyre Hall has been improved upon by each succeeding generation of Eyre's descendants. Around 1760, Eyre added a three-story, gambrel-roofed wing to the west of the original house and raised the roof on the 1730s house to a full two stories. An open colonnade was added to the east of this new structure and a Federal kitchen added later to the east end of the colonnade.

A large side hall extends from front to rear at the west end of the house in the three-story, gambrel-roofed section. The hall is divided by an elliptical central arch that separates the space into an entrance hall and a stair hall at the back. A back door out of the stair hall section affords a wonderful view of the boxwood gardens behind the house.

The walls of the stair hall are paneled with heart pine on the lower half, and above the chair rail is a beautiful French scenic wallpaper, *Les Rives de Bosphorous*, or "Banks of the Bosphorous," produced in 1816 by Dufour in Paris. The paper was printed in twenty-two-inch squares, backed with linen and mounted on plaster.

To the east of the entrance hall is the main parlor. Above the mantel is a portrait of Severn Eyre, painted by Benjamin West. (An American, West was appointed in 1772 as the official court painter for King George III of England.) Off the stair hall is the library. A Thomas Sully copy of the West portrait of Severn Eyre hangs over the mantel here. No one today seems to

Left: A screened porch off the main hall looks west over Cherrystone Creek, which runs into the Chesapeake Bay.

know why Sully, himself a renowned portraitist, made the copy of another's work.

Both the library and the parlor have doors leading to a smaller Federal entrance hall to the east. At the rear of this square hall is another door, a portal to the narrow hall that connects the east wing to the west. At the end of the hall is the dining room and off it a narrow and steep stair which leads up to bedrooms on the second floor. This older, western section of the house is one room deep–a common Colonial building style that allowed for enhanced air circulation during the hot and humid Tidewater summers.

Eyre Hall's once-open colonnade was enclosed in the 1930s and recently was remodeled into a bright, modern kitchen. The original kitchen at the east end of the colonnade has been turned into an office and storage space.

Outbuildings remaining from the eighteenth and early nineteenth century add greatly to the overall beauty of Eyre Hall. Behind the house, to the west of the gardens, are the ruins of a brick orangery built in 1819. The soft, local bricks of the orangery glow a mellow salmon color in the setting sun. Now a place of crumbling beauty, the orangery once provided the Eyres with fresh lemons and oranges. Originally two rooms, the south wall and ceiling of the orangery were glass. Across the center hall to the north is a room with three fireplaces that kept the structure warm.

Behind the orangery is the family cemetery. One grave stands out among all the old family graves. It is the grave of an itinerant musician who stopped by Eyre Hall one day, but ended up staying twenty years until his death in 1811. The gravestone doesn't give a date of birth, as no one seems to have thought to ask the musician when he was born.

Above: A finely detailed picket fence runs the length of the house, which is configured in typical Eastern Shore fashion—big house, little house, colonnade, and kitchen.

Below left: A Thomas Sully copy of a Benjamin West portrait of Severn Eyre hangs above the Federal black marble fireplace in the library.

Below right: The sun sets over Cherrystone Creek.

Littleton Eyre built
Eyre Hall on land
patented to his
grandfather and
great uncles by
Governor Berkeley
in 1662.

At the east end of the house, near the original kitchen, stands an eighteenth-century smokehouse and a dairy. The smokehouse contains the original troughs, carved from hollowed trees, that were used for salting meat. The cove molding on the eaves of the dairy has an unusual curved shape. The ventilation work near the top of the dairy is made of open "S" slats that add beauty to an otherwise simple building.

Today, H. Furlong Baldwin, a direct descendant of Eyre, is the tenth generation of his family to live on the property. In 1990, two hundred years after John Eyre laid out the garden, Baldwin added his own touch by planting English flower borders in two sections of the garden. Divided into a series of outdoor rooms, the garden contains massive boxwood hedges near the house. Beyond the boxwood garden are areas with deep perennial borders and paths lined with crape myrtles thirty feet tall and 150 years old. The entire garden is surrounded by a wall of ballast bricks.

Baldwin enjoys gardening, hunting, and sailing at Eyre Hall. He grew up at Eyre Hall, spending boyhood weekends and summers on the Eastern Shore. Today, Baldwin spends his work week in Baltimore and he rarely misses a weekend at Eyre Hall.

"As a whole," says Baldwin, "the place is comfortable and familiar. Each time I enter a room I see things I've seen a million times before, but I notice them in a different way."

Above left: The sunny yellow upstairs hall opens onto a porch that faces west toward Cherrystone Creek.

Below left: The dining room furnishings, china, and utensils are used today as in generations past.

Above: A view of Eyre Hall from Cherrystone Creek shows, to the left, the orangery built in 1819.

Left: Period poster beds and a vernacular wall paper pattern transport guests back in time.

Below: A path through towering boxwood hedges leads to the flower gardens.

Above: A Federal breakfront in the library holds a writing desk and a collection of rare books.

Right: The stair hall is decorated with the French scenic wallpaper "Banks of the Bosphorous," produced in 1816 by Dutour.

Little River Farm

Life often presents unexpected changes. So it was for Arch and Jane Edwards, the owners of Little River Farm in Louisa County, who in 1975 purchased this fifty-acre Piedmont farm. At the time it was nothing more than a ramshackle mid-eighteenth century house and some scattered outbuildings. Today, Little River Farm is an immaculately restored, middle-class plantation surrounded by fields and woods.

Little River Farm was originally the home of planter Cleavers Duke, who moved to Louisa County from neighboring Hanover County sometime after 1745 and built the house around 1750. The mid-eighteenth century marked the infancy of Louisa County, which had been formed from a severed section of Hanover County in 1742. In fact, Louisa County was on the edge of Virginia's frontier when settlers like Duke obtained their land patents.

By 1765, more than sixty-eight percent of the available land in Louisa County had been patented. Seventy percent of the farms were comprised of between 100 and 600 acres and the main crops grown were tobacco, wheat, corn, and oats. Duke's plantation boasted 700 acres, the house, and several outbuildings, all of which Duke left to his son Cosby Duke in 1763. After his death around 1775, Cosby's house passed to his widow, who lived at Little River Farm until she died in 1822.

In 1825, the house was sold outside the Duke family and was passed to a succession of apparently unrelated families. In 1870, it became the home of a Mrs. Werner-Lohman, who in 1934 left the house and 420 adjoining acres to her adopted son, Danny Reidlebach.

Little is recorded of Reidlebach's treatment of the property, but by 1965, much of the surrounding land had been sold and subdivided. When the house was purchased in 1975 by David Newhall III,

Right: Hand-hewn wooden beams in the guest cottage reveal masterful eighteenth-century craftsmanship.

who responded to an ad he had seen in the *Washington Post*, all that remained of Little River Farm was the house, outbuildings, and fifty acres. The house had been unoccupied for ten years. That same year, Edwards, a Princeton classmate of Newhall, bought the house and he and his wife began the painstaking process of restoration.

Despite changing hands so many times, the house retains its original woodwork, including raised paneled wainscotting, mantels, a built-in corner cupboard, and a paneled over-mantel in the parlor. The Edwards did little to alter the floor plan or architectural details of the house as they found it, except to add dormer windows and a bathroom upstairs. But the Edwards suspect previous owners were more liberal with their changes. Now a center-hall structure, the house is three feet wider to the left of the front door than it is to the right. The Edwards believe this lack of symmetry suggests that the house was originally built with a side hall and added to by one of the farm's several owners.

Whatever the original plan, Little River Farm today is elegant in its simplicity. The central hall downstairs runs from the front to the back of the house, opening to porches on both ends. On the ground floor, a large parlor is found to the left of the central hall with the dining room to the right. The parlor has distinctive, white-painted paneling below the chair rail. In contrast to the parlor, the dining room's paneling has been painted a chocolate brown to coordinate with a brown-hued historic Winterthur wallpaper pattern. The enclosed central stairs lead from the center hall upstairs to two bedrooms tucked under the eaves.

Across the back lawn at the farm is a red clapboard cottage used by the Edwards as a guest cottage. The original brick floor and the handhewn beams are exposed and reveal the beautiful craftsmanship in this eighteenth-century building.

"When we first saw the house in 1975, it had two electrical outlets, no plumbing, and no heat," Arch Edwards said. "Plaster was hanging loose from the lath, and termites had eaten one corner support beam in the parlor."

Left: Kitchen furnishings include an English pine table from the 1840s as well as a Smith & Son English wall clock.

Above: A portrait of Arch Edwards hangs over an English eighteenth-century oak sideboard in the cheerful blue-green parlor.

Left: The dining room table is surrounded by copies of chairs found at Hope Plantation in North Carolina.

The house retains its original woodwork, including raised paneled wainscotting, mantels, a built-in corner cupboard, and a paneled over-mantel in the parlor.

Once begun, the Edwards' work on the house at Little River Farm went fairly quickly with the help of a local craftsman. The Edwards moved in about a year after their purchase. "Looking back you can see the tapestry of your life and how it takes place," said Jane Edwards. "This house showed us a different way of life."

When they bought Little River Farm, the Edwards were living in a northern Virginia suburb of Washington, D.C., where Arch worked as an executive in a management consulting firm. They say the contrast of the peace and quiet, the old wood, and the cool nights at their new home in the country made them fall in love with the place, which they have come to call "America's answer to England."

Little River Farm was such a welcome change from the pace of Washington, D.C., that the Edwards decided to move full time to the country. In 1983, they opened the Lords Proprietors' Inn in two nineteenth-century houses in Edenton, North Carolina, and began new careers as innkeepers.

Today, Little River Farm remains a work-in-progress, and the Edwards continue to make small changes and improvements. Although their decision to buy the place ultimately led them elsewhere, they say their love for the house is unaltered.

We would not be in Edenton now if we hadn't bought this house," Jane said. Arch adds, "The house has become too important to us, our children, and grandchildren to give it up. Little River Farm has a lot of our heart in it, and we still consider it home." Several times a year the family gathers at Little River Farm to celebrate holidays and special occasions. ✒

Right: Little River Farm's white clapboards and painted tin roof are typical of early Virginia farmhouses.

Mansfield

Mansfield is part of a colonial American success story. Roger Atkinson came to America from Cumberland, England, in 1750, eager and optimistic about the life that lay ahead. Settling in Dinwiddie County to the west of Petersburg on the Appomattox River, the twenty-five-year-old entrepreneur bought about 1,100 acres of fertile land on which he hoped to grow tobacco.

Within a decade, Atkinson had moved into an existing house on the property—a one-and-a-half-story frame structure with five bays upstairs. Believed to have been built before 1750, the house was four rooms wide and one room deep, with two rooms upstairs. This original house was a simple structure, but the drawing room boasted elaborate raised paneling and a deeply projecting molded cornice on the east wall.

Roger Atkinson quickly became a prominent member of his Virginia community and came to meet notable figures from the colony. In a 1774 letter to his brother-in-law Samuel Pleasants in Philadelphia, Atkinson describes some prominent fellow Virginians. "Colonel Washington was bred a soldier and a warrior. . . . A modest man, but sensible & speaks little—in action cool, like a Bishop at his prayers." About Patrick Henry he observed, ". . . moderate & mild & in religious matters a Saint, but ye very Devil in Politicks. . . ." Roger Atkinson also served on the vestry of Bristol Parish from 1760 until his death in 1784.

As Atkinson's fortunes grew, so did his house. Around 1780, he added a connecting hyphen with an open-string stair and a two-story wing to the north. The downstairs room

Left: The exposed brick fireplace wall in the dining room provides a perfect backdrop for the Guthrie's kitchen collection.

Insurance policies taken out by Roger Atkinson's heir Robert Atkinson in 1802 and 1805 describe the house much as it is in its present form.

Above: Dogwood, the Virginia state flower, blooms abundantly at Mansfield.

Left: The original part of Mansfield was built sometime before 1750.

of this wing, twenty-two by twenty-eight feet, served as a ballroom and still contains raised-panel wainscotting with an asymmetrical chair rail and tiers of small panels above it. The chimney breast projects deeply into the ballroom and is intersected by an unusual center beam that runs the length of the ceiling. Above the ballroom, Atkinson built a large master bedroom. Because of his serial building, Atkinson's rooms boast varying ceiling heights and general proportions.

Each view of Mansfield's exterior is also different. The north wing gives the house a T-shape. Yet facing the original front or south side, it is difficult to see beyond the steeply pitched hipped roof to the two-story wing to the north. Today, the main entrance to the house is from the west through the hyphen stair hall.

Insurance policies taken out by Roger Atkinson's heir Robert Atkinson in 1802 and 1805 describe the house much as it is in its present form, with a kitchen to the west and a large washing house to the east. Sometime in the 1830s, Mansfield became a girls' school run by Hugh A. Garland. By 1905, Mansfield had been bought by William B. McIlwaine, an Atkinson descendant. McIlwaine repaired and remodeled the house and installed the present doors, ground-story flooring, kitchen, and a bell system. The house went through a series of owners before it was purchased in the early 1970s by the Henshaws, a Dinwiddie County family.

In November 1980, Carl and Bettie Guthrie purchased Mansfield and began a two-year renovation that required the Guthries to set up housekeeping the first winter with two woodstoves and no kitchen. The Guthries worked on the house one room

Left: A reflecting pool is a focal point for tranquil contemplation in the Mansfield garden.

Right: In the 1780s stair hall is a marble-topped table purchased at auction in Petersburg.

at a time and did much of the restoration themselves. The Guthrie's three children, now all grown, loved the quirky aspects of the house—like the extra-wide front door. Called a "funeral door," it was designed to allow the entry of a coffin with pallbearers on each side in the days when the dead were viewed at home before burial.

The Guthries weren't put off by the eccentricities of their house. "We'd always wanted to restore an old home," says Bettie Guthrie. "Carl probably looked at 100 homes during one year alone." Mr. Guthrie grew up in New Bern, North Carolina, a coastal town known for its old homes, and saw Mansfield as his ultimate challenge.

Every room except the kitchen has a fireplace. The kitchen is located in a room that was added to the west of the dining room behind its fireplace. Bettie Guthrie was hoping for a fireplace in the kitchen and during the restoration began chipping away at the plaster around the chimney in that room—only to be disappointed.

Mansfield has offered the Guthries few other disappointments. "We have loved living here," says Bettie Guthrie. "It was great having the canal down along the river for the kids to canoe in and places nearby where my husband could hunt." Like Roger Atkinson, the Guthries have succeeded in finding just what they were looking for—a place to call home. ❧

Right: The ballroom, said to be one of the largest rooms in Dinwiddie County, is filled with old family pieces and handmade furniture, and is divided down its center by an unusual ceiling beam.

Mount Airy

DRIVE SLOWLY
TO AVOID RAISING
DUST. WHICH DRAWS
SHELL FIRE

Skeptics cautioned Colonel John Tayloe II when he chose soft, local sandstone to build Mount Airy in 1758, saying the house wouldn't stand for twenty-five years. The Colonel proved his naysayers wrong. Even as some of his detractors' wooden homes have perished, Mount Airy has endured despite 200 years of wind, rain, and fires. And the Tayloe family, who still reside at Mount Airy, fully expects their house to last another century or two.

Mount Airy is the work of noted architect John Ariss (1725-1799), who also designed Mount Vernon, Kenmore in Fredericksburg, Carlyle House in Alexandria, and Fairfield in Clarke County. Trained in England, the American-born Ariss returned to the colonies in 1751, advertising in the *Maryland Gazette* as an architect and builder. "John Ariss (lately from Great Britain) Buildings of all Sorts and Dimensions are undertaken and performed in the neatest Manner (and at cheaper rates). . . ." For Mount Airy, Ariss took his inspiration from Haddo House in Aberdeenshire, Scotland, but his building materials were quarried right on

Above: Curved hyphens connecting symmetrical wings give Mount Airy's forecourt the look of an English Georgian manor house.

the plantation.

The walls of the main house are made of sandstone three feet thick, with architectural trim of a light-colored limestone from nearby Aquia Creek. The Palladian facade with curved hyphens and the attached dependencies form the forecourt that gives Mount Airy the look of a villa—quite a departure from the typical austere Colonial plantation home.

The main building at Mount Airy has pedimented pavilions on the front and back in a style of stonework often called "rusticated." Horizontal and vertical channels cut in the joints exaggerate the limestone coursework.

Mount Airy is a last-second surprise for approaching visitors who may expect to find a simple Colonial house. After following a winding drive, guests first view the house from the side and walk onto a terraced forecourt. The front walkway leads to a recessed loggia with four Doric columns. There the front door is flanked by two floor-to-ceiling windows that draw light, as well as guests, into the great hall. Now used as a drawing room, the twenty-by-thirty-foot hall, with fourteen-foot ceilings, offers an imposing first impression. To the west of the great hall is the dining room with its walls covered by numerous

Left: A view from the garden shows the roof stack of one of four interior chimneys.

Above: Unusual hand-beaten brass surrounds decorate several of the fireplaces at Mount Airy.

Right: The great hall also serves as the main parlor. On the walls hang several family portraits, part of one of the largest collections of its kind.

Overleaf left: Eighteenth- and nineteenth-century furnishings are combined to charming effect in a downstairs guest room.

Overleaf right: More family portraits hang in the dining room. The sideboard holds pieces from the family's collection of Chinese export "Rouge de Fer" (iron-red) china.

family portraits; Mount Airy is said to have the largest collection of family portraits of any private home in the United States.

Leading off the great hall to the east is a smaller hall that ends with a large Palladian window and doors into the downstairs guest bedroom and the library. In that same hallway is a rare 1850s cylinder piano that appears to be a cross between a spinet piano and a secretary. It is reported that Union soldiers stopped to play this instrument when they took possession of the house during the Civil War. Pleased to hear "Yankee Doodle," family members say the soldiers left Mount Airy undisturbed. Other family treasures include Chippendale dining chairs and a Chinese Chippendale marble-topped table.

Tayloes have been around this region since the early days of the Colonies. In 1650, a member of the family patented 6,000 acres of Rappahannock River forestland that eventually became the site of Mount Airy. Related to several other families in the vicinity, the Tayloes include among their kin the Carters of Sabine Hall (see page 102) and the Lees of Stratford Hall. In 1769, Rebecca, daughter of John Tayloe II, married Francis Lightfoot Lee, a signer of the Declaration of Independence. Rebecca and Francis Lee lived at Mount Airy while her father built them a home called Menokin on a nearby plantation. The couple are buried in the Tayloe family graveyard at Mount Airy.

The house passed through seven generations of Tayloes before the current owner's husband, H. Gwynne Tayloe, inherited Mount Airy in 1964 from his elderly aunt. Mrs. Tayloe and her late husband made Mount Airy comfortable without compromising its history. Although the house was nearly ruined by a fire in the 1840s that gutted the main structure, the sandstone exterior withstood the heat, and the walls and woodwork were restored with mid-nineteenth-century detailing.

The attached dependencies were untouched by the fire, and today the curved hyphen leading to the west dependency is Mrs. Tayloe's kitchen. Looking much like a ship's galley, the modern kitchen is adjacent to the unrestored Colonial kitchen in the west dependency. Used for storage, the Colonial kitchen stands complete with its original open fireplace and pots hanging from iron cranes. Mrs. Tayloe's daughter and grandchildren now live in the restored east dependency.

Other extant outbuildings include the stables. Once known as an outstanding horse racing and breeding stable, Mount Airy was home to many thoroughbred champions. Both John Tayloe II and III were well-known on the colonial American racing scene. John Tayloe III is said to have played an important role in the development of the American thoroughbred through his experiments with breeding. He owned several winning horses, including Yorick, Selima, and Castianira, the dam of Sir Archy. From 1791 until his retirement in 1806, John Tayloe III was acknowledged by many to be America's premier horseman.

Mount Airy represents the best in Colonial architecture. The Tayloes continue to value the rich history and outstanding architecture of their home, and the unrestored portions of the house offer future generations a chance to imprint their own style on the place. Chances are the three-foot-thick sandstone walls of Mount Airy will allow another 200 years of Tayloes to walk its glorious halls.

Left: Elaborate stone finials flank the steps in the front forecourt.

Right: A medicine chest rests on a mid-eighteenth century table in the great hall.

Rocketts Mill Farm

Above: The informal dining room in the English basement has stone floors laid by the owner during the latest renovations at Rocketts Mill.

Built solidly into the side of a hill overlooking the New Found River, Rocketts Mill Farm presents an intriguing facade for those who, on a sunny day, drive by on the country road that winds to the west of the property: the imposing white-painted brick house fairly gleams against the green hillside.

Thomas Price, a relative of the Prices of Cool Water (see page 46) built the house in 1735 just one hundred yards above the falls of the New Found, a beautiful setting as well as a strategic one. In 1781,

the Marquis de Lafayette used Rocketts as a temporary headquarters before retreating from British General Cornwallis. A few days after Lafayette's departure, Cornwallis moved into the house. Later, Polish General Casimir Pulaski used the house for the better part of a week as his command post. A few bullet holes and scars in the west wall attest to some firing, mostly with small arms, upon the house, but the Revolutionary back-and-forth was more to the preserving of Rocketts than to its destruction.

Rocketts Mill was one of the grander homes in eighteenth century Hanover County and it remains so today. The simple but impressive side-gabled, Georgian home rises three full stories from an English basement. Two side chimneys serve six fireplaces in the twelve-room house. The entire basement lies below this level and opens out to the sloping hillside to the north (or back) of the house.

Guests in the 1790s would have approached the house from the south, or front, side, which faces a level lawn studded with old walnut, elm, and cedar trees. Although the approach was altered when a modern road connected the farm to the west, then as now, guests are greeted in a large center hall that runs from the front to the back of the house. A simple but beautiful stairway rises along the east wall. The wide treads and risers are made of heart pine, while the rails and newel post are of mahogany. To the west of the hall through a wide door is the large, twenty-seven-foot-square parlor.

The heart of Rocketts Mill is this parlor. Here four, recessed, eighteen-pane windows (two on each side) flood the room with light from both the south and north. The parlor fireplace is made from heart poplar, and carved with fluted columns and a beaded shelf facing. Two other fireplaces at Rocketts Mill are similarly crafted in heart poplar. The remaining three fireplaces boast simpler and somewhat heavier columns and shelves, and are made from heart pine.

At the back of the hall to the east and behind the staircase is a door leading into the living room. During the eighteenth century, this room most likely had another use. For that matter, the dining room may once have been in the English basement.

Right: A view of the house from the river below.

In 1781, the Marquis de Lafayette used Rocketts Mill as a temporary headquarters before retreating from British General Cornwallis. A few days after Lafayette's departure, Cornwallis moved into the house.

Left: The main hall opens to a screened porch with a view of the New Found River.

Above: Enormous lilacs attract monarch and swallowtail butterflies.

99

Overall, little is known about how the rooms at Rocketts were used during its first 250 years, and the history of ownership at Rocketts Mill is likewise sketchy. The house remained in the Price family for many years and, at one point before 1820, was owned by a William Timberlake. The popular history ends there until the 20th century. During the Civil War, Hanover County records were taken to Richmond for safekeeping. During the evacuation of Richmond in 1865, the records–as well as those of several other counties–were destroyed by fire, the ownership documents of Rocketts Mill among them. Early in this century, the house was purchased by a C. Lukaszkleivicz and, in the late 1960s, the house and surrounding farm was bought by Ed Stevens and his wife.

Stevens, a breeder and trainer of thoroughbred horses, has trained dozens of stakes winners at Rocketts Mill Farm. The rolling, mineral-rich land at Rocketts Mill provides an ideal setting for a thoroughbred horse operation, he says.

Thirty years ago, the house at Rocketts Mill Farm was still solid but in need of renovation. All repairs to the house, including framing, joists, and sills, are rip sawn or hand hewn, and wooden pegs or blacksmiths nails were used throughout the house to secure the refurbished woodwork. The broken and crumbling floors in the two large rooms in the English basement were replaced with stone and brick. Stevens jacked up the dividing wall in the center of the basement and turned all the bricks around to expose old, but more attractive faces. On the east end of the house, Stevens added a shed wing with a modern kitchen and a sunroom. Upstairs bedrooms were modernized and bathrooms were added. Yet, essentially, the house remains the same as it did 260 years ago when Thomas Price built it.

Like many before him, Stevens was intrigued by the house when he drove by it one day. "I liked the look of the house," he says. "I have loved living here and our three children were happy growing up here."

Right: The dining room table is set with a combination of English and American antique china. The gleaming silver bowls and cups on the mantel are trophies honoring the Stevens' many horse racing victories.

Sabine Hall

Robert "King" Carter was the quintessential colonial planter, the richest man in Virginia—and probably in the colonies—during the late 1600s and early 1700s. King lived up to his name. Not only was he a vastly successful merchant and planter, but he was also a force as a shipper and boatbuilder, as a stockman and storeowner, as a moneylender, and as a shrewd investor. He would see his children and grandchildren marry into nearly every prominent family in Virginia, and he founded a family dynasty that would include two U.S. presidents and two signers of the Declaration of Independence. Upon his death in 1732, Carter's fortune consisted of dozens of plantations and more than 300,000 acres of land. Four of those pieces of land were on the banks of the Rappahannock across the river from the port of Hobbs' Hole (today, the town of Tappahannock). Left by King Carter to his son Landon, those four farms would form the nucleus of Sabine Hall Plantation.

Sometime around 1740, Landon Carter built his elegant Georgian dwelling high on a hill that looked southward (from where the piazza is today) over six terraced gardens to the Rappahannock River three miles below. This new Carter family seat and surrounding plantation he named Sabine Hall—reportedly after the sheltered "sabine vale" in the hills near Rome that Horace described in his poem Contentment—where he could live "undisturbed by the rush for fame."

One can almost envision Landon Carter walking on his covered piazza on the south face at Sabine Hall. He wrote in his diary on February 14, 1774: "I walked a mile this day. . . and find I'm strong in doing it. . . ." The piazza afforded him a view of his vast plantation as well as a way to stay out of the rain while he took his exercise.

Landon Carter and seven generations of Carters and Wellfords since have enjoyed the peaceful setting of Sabine Hall and the 4,000 acres of farmland and marshland that surround it still. According to colonial Tidewater custom, Landon Carter designed Sabine Hall himself. As self-taught architects, the Virginia aristocracy of the eighteenth century sought to combine indigenous architectural style

Above: The parlor holds many family pieces, including the highboy flanked by the front windows.

Left: Above the fireplace in this small parlor called "Landon's Office" hangs a portrait of Landon Carter, who built this house at Sabine Hall plantation.

Sabine Hall has undergone various architectural changes over its 250 years, including the addition of a two-story Greek Revival porch in the 1830s.

Above: Beautiful coordinated fabrics drape the furnishings of this first-floor guest room located just off the stair hall.

Right: A view of the front (or land side) of the house shows the Greek Revival porch added in the 1830s by Robert Wormley Carter II.

with grand traditions. Landon Carter accomplished this goal, at least in part, when he designed the great halls on the first and second floors. They are spectacular, light-filled rooms from which the other main rooms radiate. Off the great hall to the southwest are a parlor and dining room and to the southeast are a study and a guest bedroom divided by a separate stair hall. The walls of the downstairs great hall are hung with family portraits, including one of patriarch King Carter, which serves to remind visitors of the colonial power of the family.

A politically and socially powerful man in his own right, Landon Carter concerned himself with more than architecture and farming. A prolific author and recognized authority on the topic of medicine, Carter wrote frequently on this subject and even attempted to assist his family and slaves with their medical needs. He discussed one of his most acclaimed attempts in his journal. Upon learning that one of his slaves had been struck unconscious by lightning, Landon revived the man by blowing into his mouth with the fireplace bellows—an unorthodox but ingenious treatment which seems to have saved the man's life. His journal entries are filled with records of his medical research and experiments, and include as well his design for the construction of the piazza where he might have his regular exercise.

Landon Carter's descendants have done little to change the inside of the 1740s portion of the house, leaving the rooms configured much as Carter had originally designed them. Upon entering the downstairs great hall from the north, visitors can look southward through the house and out the piazza doors to the gardens and river. The great hall was an important public room in Landon Carter's time. Today, the parlors and the dining room off the central hall are much-used areas for entertaining. Family weddings are still held on the front lawn and, in season, hunting parties make frequent weekend gatherings.

Other parts of the house have undergone varying degrees of architectural change, including the lowering of the original Georgian roof and the addition, by Robert Wormley Carter II, of a columned Greek Revival porch (on the side away from the river) in the 1830s. In the 1920s, the

house was left to Armistead Nelson Wellford II and William Harrison Wellford I, sons of Robert Carter Wellford I (the first Wellford to own Sabine Hall). The brothers decided to construct a new, comparably proportioned northwest wing and operate the two wings as independent and separate households.

More modest changes have been made to the formal eighteenth-century English garden laid out by Landon Carter on the second terrace. Designed with gravel paths in a symmetrical pattern, the features of the northwest side are a mirror image of those on the southeast. On the third terrace, originally used for the cultivation of fruit, a few vestiges of trees remain.

Over all, little has changed at Sabine Hall over the past 250 years. It is still a working farm and Carter descendants still live in the house. In fact, a unique living arrangement exists at Sabine Hall. The southeast wing is owned by Robert Carter Wellford III, while his cousin Beverley Randolph Wellford lives in the northwest wing. The cousins refer to the house as their "eighteenth-century duplex." Of the original ten rooms built by Landon Carter, they share the central great halls upstairs and downstairs, with the remaining eight rooms divided evenly between the southeast and northwest wings. Both families use the main staircase in the great halls. Beverley's wife, Joyce Wellford, describes the arrangement: "It's a very pleasant experience and we've always gotten along extremely well."

Today's owners of Sabine Hall live comfortably with the past. As one climbs the well-worn steps of the beautiful transverse corridor staircase off the great hall, with its turned walnut balusters and side-pegged original heart pine floors, one senses the spirit of colonial patriots. This feeling is confirmed upon entering the "George Washington bedroom," so named by the family for its famous overnight guest. Much of the furniture and silver has been at Sabine Hall from its beginning or has been returned to the house by various generations of Carters who wish to provide furnishings and historical continuity to their home. As Joyce Wellford describes her philosophy about Sabine Hall, "we aren't really owners of a house like this, rather we are stewards."

Left: Greek busts flank the front door in the great hall.

Right: The main staircase is hewn from heart pine and complemented with walnut balusters.

Above: A family portrait hangs in the front hall over an eighteenth-century tapestry chair that once provided seating in Prince Hohenlohe's palace in Austerlitz, Austria.

Westover, an elegant Georgian plantation home, has earned its place in the annals of American colonial architecture. The home's distinctive front doorway with its Portland stone surrounds has given a unique style to architects and designers—the Westover door—a style emulated in grand homes throughout the United States.

William Byrd II, who built Westover around 1730, selected simple lines for the main structure of the house and embellished it with rich details on the doors, windows, and gates. Byrd used pattern books to design the house—a common practice in colonial America—but Byrd's own sense of design and style took Westover a few steps further. The house is more elaborate than most pattern-book houses and clearly bears Byrd's individual architectural stamp. The main gate is widely known as one of America's finest examples of early wrought-iron crafting, and the lead eagles on the gateposts are believed to have been designed to be emblematic of the name "Byrd."

Born in 1678, William Byrd II was not simply a prominent citizen of colonial Virginia, but was also the founder of the cities of Richmond and Petersburg. Like many colonial aristocrats, he was educated in England, where he no doubt was exposed to the grandeur of English country houses. Byrd returned to an active life in Virginia business and politics, and, when he was twenty-eight, inherited Westover from his father, William Byrd I, who had purchased the property from Richard Bland in 1688.

Although another house existed on the plantation, the younger Byrd decided to undertake the construction of a grand manor home that would make Westover famous. He chose a building site close to the north bank of the James River in Charles City County. His neighbors—the Carters, the Harrisons, and the Tylers—all had established family seats along the river and two of these families would later produce U.S. presidents. Today, this area along the north side of the James River is known for its historic plantation homes still lived in by the descendants of those first families.

From the river, a grove of centuries-old tulip poplars stands on the south lawn of Byrd's grand design. The three-story house supported a steeply sloping slate roof with tall paired chimneys at each end. The two wings originally were identical, separate buildings set perpendicular to the main house. The overall effect was one of elegance, substance, and simplicity.

During the Civil War, fire destroyed the east wing, taking with it Byrd's library of more than 4,000 volumes. Sometime around 1900, the wing was rebuilt, and both wings were then attached to the house.

Byrd apparently was determined for Westover to excel both indoors and out. He designed a large hall that runs south to north through the center of the

Above: A pier at Westover is reflected in the calm waters of the James River.

Above left: An eighteenth-century Austrian Empire desk stands between the windows in the dining room.

Right: Canopy beds await guests in an upstairs bedroom.

Today, this area along the north side of the James River in Charles City County is known for its historic plantation homes.

house. The ceiling of the hall is decorated with plaster flowers in the French Rococo style. On the west side of this hall is a wide staircase, with an elaborately carved mahogany balustrade and stringers, which rises all the way to the third floor. Two cuts on the newel post of the stairs are said to have been made by Benedict Arnold in 1781 when he was at Westover with the British army. Arnold rode his horse into the front hall and stuck his saber into the newel to rouse the family.

From the outside, the front door appears to be in the center of the house—but it is really east of center and the window directly to the west of the door is in the hallway, allowing light into what would otherwise be a very dark room. The hall window—like all the other windows facing the James River on the first and second floors—is equipped with curious wooden blinds, constructed of two wide panels with a narrow one in the middle, apparently so they could be opened to accommodate the barrel of a gun.

To the east of the hallway are two large drawing rooms. The red drawing room, on the river side of the house, contains an unusual black Italian marble mantel. The mantel and surrounding panels rise nearly to the ceiling and incorporate a large mirror, as well as a white marble swag of fruits and leaves, an elaborate pediment, and other details. As in the hallway, the red drawing room has detailed plaster work on the ceiling, with medallions depicting Dante and Virgil.

A long dining room located to the west of the hallway has two fireplaces, indicating it was once two rooms. Through a door in the west wall of the dining room and down a few steps the current owners have built a modern galley-style kitchen in what was once the passageway to the west wing.

Left: The local hunt regularly convenes outside the famous William Byrd gates.

Right: A secret passage leads from the second-floor hall to the west wing.

On the opposite side of the house, doors lead out of each of the drawing rooms and down steps to a long room with floor-to-ceiling windows on all four sides. Through an arch at the east end of the room is a parlor with a small raised platform. Once a stage used for family entertaining, the back wall of the platform is today lined with bookcases. This wing of the house was rebuilt in the nineteenth century on the foundations of the original east wing.

Upstairs in the main house are four large bedrooms, two on each side, surrounding the center hall. Passageways lead from the hall to long dormitory-style bedrooms in both the east and west wings.

Outbuildings include a freestanding brick building near the west wing that was the original kitchen and antedates the house. There are also an ice house, stables, and other farm buildings. To the west of the house is a formal garden of colonial design that includes the tomb of William Byrd II, whose epitaph reads, "Black Swan of Westover."

The current residents of Westover, Fred and Muschi Fisher, are always mindful of the colorful history of their house. Westover was purchased by Mr. Fisher's grandfather, Richard Crane, an ambassador to Czechoslovakia during Woodrow Wilson's administration, for his southern bride, Ellen Bruce, in 1921 (see Staunton Hill, page 192). Fred Fisher's mother, Bruce Crane Fisher, was the mistress of Westover for three decades and Fred Fisher grew up in the house.

For more than fifteen years, the Fishers and their children, Andrea and Peter, have made Westover their home. "I've loved living here," says Muschi, a native of Germany. "It's so beautiful and I feel the history. I know I'm part of what has gone before."

Westover is often open for house tours, receptions, and community functions. The house has been the location of several movies, including *Dream West* starring Richard Chamberlin, *The Ironclads*, and a television pilot called *The Monroes*. "We have always felt privileged to live here," says Muschi Fisher. "We want to share Westover with the public."

Left: A portrait of Judge Anderson, Fred Fisher's great great-grandfather, hangs over the mantel in the enormous dining room.

115

Federal 1790–1830

Bracketts

Above: A portrait of Elizabeth Nolting's father, William Otto Nolting, hangs in the front hall.

Bracketts has been a Green Springs monument for nearly two hundred years. The large, clapboard farmhouse was built by John Brackett in 1805 and sold shortly thereafter to the Watsons, a family counted among the very early settlers of western Louisa County and noteworthy as pillars in Green Springs society. Green Springs, a roughly 14,000-acre tract, was settled in the early 1800s when its distinctive, highly fertile soil became apparent to homesteaders, as well as the gently rolling hills that supplied both easy drainage and a bounty of natural beauty.

Green Springs society converged when James Watson of Bracketts married his first cousin, Susan Dabney Morris of Sylvania, in 1831. Twelve years after her husband's death in 1837, Susan Morris Watson decided to build her own home at the western edge of Bracketts farm on land her husband had left her. She called her new home Westend (see page 200). Bracketts remained in the Watson family until around 1900, when it was purchased by Carl Nolting, a Morris relative and Virginia's Game Commissioner. Throughout the last

century and into this one, the two families have continued to work the land of Green Springs and to support each other, their holdings connected by a postern gate and separated by only the simplest of field fences.

Bracketts has, over the years, seen several changes and additions and is now at the centerpiece of a thriving farmstead. The main section of the house was probably built on the side hall plan with a double parlor to the west of the front hall. The house has varying ceiling heights and incorporates several architectural styles throughout its interior. From the outside, it is easy to see the Victorian influence in the bracketed cornices and window trim. The arches in the recessed windows of the back parlor and the beautiful heart pine paneling below the chair rail in the hallway and parlors show the attention to craftsmanship by the original builder of the house. To the right of the front hall is a low-ceilinged sitting room that might have been part of an earlier house joined to the main house. The kitchen was originally located in an outbuilding that is still on the property.

To the west of the main house is a twenty-five acre pond that is popular with local fishermen, who must follow the rules of fishing etiquette posted near the house. Between the main house and the pond is a cottage that was built in the 1780s and moved to its present location. The main house, cottage, and assorted outbuildings form the nucleus of a still active and prosperous farm.

That prosperity had been seriously threatened in the early 1970s when Green Springs residents battled developers who first wanted to build a prison at Green Springs and later wanted to mine there for vermiculite. The threats were challenged by the grassroots opposition of Green Springs's residents, lead by Elizabeth Nolting, the owner of Bracketts. She organized the homeowners of the

Left: A nineteenth-century pump organ stands ready to be played in the front hall.

Right: The south side of the house reveals an elegant combination of architectural styles.

Green Springs has been designated—thanks to Elizabeth Nolting of Bracketts—a National Historic Landmark District.

Above: Original brick outbuildings, including an old kitchen, date from the same period as the main house.

Left: The twenty-acre, man-made lake near the house was dug in the 1920s.

Right: An enormous gilt mirror in the parlor was originally in the Nolting-Hobson house in Richmond, the childhood home of Elizabeth Nolting, that was razed in the 1940s.

area and succeeded in having Green Springs designated a National Historic Landmark District, making it one of the few agricultural areas in the country with such a designation.

The historic district is comprised of nearly half of the 14,000 acres of land and thirty-five historic properties, including houses, churches, and a Colonial tavern. Altogether, Green Springs represents an outstanding assemblage of rural Virginia architecture from colonial times to the 1860s.

Today, homeowners like the Noltings at Bracketts seek to preserve the past while developing farming traditions for the future. Elizabeth's cousin, George Nolting, has returned to Virginia after twenty-five years in California, and is studying a variety of ways to make farming at Bracketts sustainable and environmentally safe. Among his farm projects are an organic garden, an effort to make paper from local Mulberry trees, and a cattle operation that involves natural grazing.

George Nolting is quick to remind visitors that he wants to farm without compromising the habits and habitats of local wildlife. To perpetuate Bracketts as a symbol for preservation, the Noltings have formed a foundation which now owns the house and the surrounding property. With the Noltings foresight and careful planning, Bracketts will continue to be at the center of Green Springs life for many generations. ❧

Left: A desk in the upstairs hall is laden with family photos and pictures of favorite horses.

Right: In the dining room in the southwest corner of the house, the table is set with Nolting family Limoge china.

Farley

Above: The clapboard exterior of Farley is at once imposing and inviting.

First-time visitors to Farley rarely expect what they find at this Piedmont plantation. The house, built in the early 1800s, stands atop a wooded knoll, perfectly framed by the foothills of the Blue Ridge mountains. Here the imposing, ninety-six-foot-long Palladian facade of painted, cream-colored clapboards makes a dazzling picture, not only because of its grand size, but also for the choice of wood over brick as the building material for this stately Georgian design.

Farley—built in 1802 by William Champe Carter, the sixth son of Edward Carter of Blenheim—was surely a significant home in the wilderness of Culpeper County. Carter came to this area of Virginia in 1805 from the much-civilized Albemarle County, and bought the land on which Farley stands from Robert Beverley, Jr. The land had been part of a 2,000-acre grant patented in 1792 by Lord Fairfax to Robert Beverley of Blandfield in Essex County (see

Blandfield, page 30). Robert Beverley had named the estate Sans Souci (probably for the circa 1745 palace of Frederick II) and had left it and his other holdings to his son Robert Beverley, Jr. Carter set right to work on his new property, completing the prodigious frame structure a year later and naming it for his wife, Maria Byrd Farley.

In 1834, Carter died much in debt and, within several years, his widow was forced to sell the plantation. The house, furniture, about a thousand books, plantation implements, and forty slaves were valued at $11,000 and sold lock, stock, and barrel to William N. Wellford in April 1843. In 1863, Wellford sold Farley to Franklin P. Stearns, Sr., in whose family the estate remained—although not always in habitable condition—until 1978.

During the Civil War, the house was appropriated by Union troops. Here Union General John Sedgwick was headquartered prior to action at the nearby battle of Brandy Station, the largest cavalry battle fought in the Western Hemisphere. Sedgwick and his troops were captured on the steps at Farley in a photograph by Matthew Brady. After the Civil War, Farley gradually fell into disrepair and was ultimately abandoned until, in 1986, the house was sold to C.D. Ward, who has completely restored the historic home.

Farley's grand facade opens to a simple, even provincial interior. Constructed on a modified E-shaped plan, the house has been characterized by some architectural historians as an elaborate log cabin. After entering the front door on the south side of the house, guests step into a large, rectangular hall that runs to the back of the house. Radiating from the central hall are two lateral halls that extend east and west across the front side of the house and end in dog-leg stairs. Down the west lateral hall are doors leading into the dining room and kitchen, while to the east are the library and the parlor. The south passageway is more than seventy-five feet long and is lined with ten windows.

Upstairs, one long hall across the south side of the house connects four bedrooms to the master suite. Eight windows in the upstairs hall provide warm, southern light, and a

Above: A brass and iron lock demonstrates the marriage of form and function.

Right: The library is filled with treasures from around the world. Among them, on the far wall, is a painting of General Kearney, who liberated Santa Fe during the Mexican-American War in the 1840s.

Union General
John Sedgwick
and his troops
were captured in a
photograph by
Matthew Brady
on the steps
at Farley.

Above left: Buttercups abound in Farley's fields each spring.

*Below left: The modern upstairs bathroom was built in
what was once a storage room.*

*Right: Ten south-facing windows flood the seventy-five-foot
front hall with sunlight.*

small door, with a fan-shaped window above it, opens to the covered second-floor porch. The porch, with its Chippendale-style railing, was rebuilt by the Wards after they discovered a drawing of Farley on a letter written by a Union soldier during the Civil War.

The letter was one of several historic artifacts that the Wards used in their painstaking two-year restoration of Farley. Local craftsmen helped the Wards rebuild the stone smokehouse and Dale Adler of Charlottesville spent ten months applying and restoring decorative paints to the woodwork and doors in the house. The Wards' efforts were recognized when the National Trust for Historic Preservation named Farley the 1991 winner for craftsmanship in the Trust's Great American Home Awards Program. The entire renovation was guided by Don A. Swofford, a Charlottesville architectural historian, who wrote his 1973 master's thesis about Farley.

"Fancypainter" Dale Adler labored for nearly a year on the painting at Farley and remembers how he spent entire days mixing and remixing paints with Sita Ward. "The primary distinction between fancypainting and faux painting is that the painter tries to think about what sort of pigments and paint materials a painter of that period might have used," says Dale Adler. He explains that fancy-painting (which was popular from about 1790 until 1840) doesn't attempt to look faux or even to replicate the exact colors that might have been used in 1805. Instead, fancypainters today attempt to use original nineteenth-century methods and palettes that will result in something inherently beautiful as well as authentic to the original period of a house.

Sita Ward used the same philosophy in decorating Farley. Not a purist about any one period or style, she has filled the house with family pieces and antiques from all over the world. This combination of styles and periods preserves the past and at the same time gives Farley its own, unique style.

The Wards' interpretation of how Farley should look is in keeping with the house William Champe Carter built more than 190 years ago on the edge of Virginia's wilderness, a house of grandeur and surprises. ⚘

Right: One of the large upstairs bedrooms provides guests with a warm fire and abundant space in which to rest and relax.

Fotheringay

Fotheringay—a name notorious in the sixteenth century as the British castle prison where Mary, Queen of Scots, was held captive for nineteen years by Elizabeth, Queen of England—was the name selected by Colonel George Hancock for his post-colonial Virginia plantation home. Built around 1795 on a steep knoll overlooking the Roanoke River and the Wilderness Trail, Hancock's Fotheringay was a less controversial home than its British namesake. But Fotheringay was well known to travelers who passed below its mountain setting just east of the trail; few could miss the imposing sight of this two-story, brick mansion with its façade of three bays. Because the portico was placed at the far southern end of the house, instead of centered, many passersby thought the house was unfinished and, as a result, dubbed Fotheringay the "half house." Others appreciated its asymmetry and considered Colonel Hancock's home one of the most elaborate and finely executed in frontier Virginia.

Hancock enjoyed rich ornaments inside and out. He adorned the front stair hall and drawing room with Adam-style decoration, including modillion and dentil cornices and swags in the entablatures over the doorways. The drawing room chimney piece is unusually ornate with its broken pediment overmantel flanked by carved scrolls.

Above: The capacious front hall is trimmed with fine moldings and an elaborately carved ceiling medallion.

Below: The north bedroom is believed to be one of the few bedrooms on the Virginia frontier that was furnished with intricate moldings and an overmantel.

Hancock's unique decorative legacy is apparent even in the upstairs front bedroom. In fact, Fotheringay is the only Federal period house in Virginia to have a "finished" bedroom, that is, one with elaborate moldings, door surrounds, and an especially fine overmantel more typical of parlors or "downstairs" rooms. No one knows exactly why Hancock took such care with the master bedroom; however, it adds greatly to the overall style of the house.

Hancock was a prominent resident of late eighteenth-century Botetourt County (today, Montgomery County). Born in nearby Fincastle in 1754, Hancock was a local attorney, aide to Count Casimir Pulaski during the American Revolution, and a member of the Third and Fourth U.S. Congresses (1793 to 1797). Many prominent people passed through Fotheringay's halls as a result. What's more, Hancock also hosted the wedding of his daughter Julia to explorer William Clark (of Lewis and Clark fame) at this venerable home.

Upon Hancock's death in 1820, Fotheringay was sold to local attorney Henry Edmundson, whose descendants, Dr. Robert Nutt and his sister Juliette Nutt Dalton, are the current owners. The house remained virtually unchanged until the 1950s, when Robert Nutt, Jr., and his wife, Sarah, decided to balance the front facade by adding two more bays to the house. Today, the house appears symmetrical, and is, of course, significantly larger than Hancock's original.

The house is L-shaped, with a drawing room to the north, off the main hall, and a library to the south in the 1950s wing. Behind the drawing room is an enormous dining room. The dining room once

Above: The dazzling Venetian chandelier was purchased by the owner's parents in Italy.

Right: Ornate exterior detailing helps make Fotheringay one of the finest post-Colonial plantation homes in southwest Virginia.

contained the back stairs, but today is a very large, rectangular room with windows on two sides. On the south side of the house, at the back, is a two-story porch and, behind the dining room, is a kitchen, pantry, and the servants' rooms.

Behind the house is the original kitchen, some orchards, and a small family cemetery. Against the base of the mountains to the east, and in view of the house, stands the triangular-shaped stone tomb of Colonel Hancock and several members of his family. Local lore says that Colonel Hancock's tomb is oddly shaped due to the fact that he was buried standing up. No one in the family can confirm this tale.

Fotheringay has played an important role in the lives of six generations of Edmundsons. During the Great Depression, Annie Edmundson, her brother Eskridge, and sister Marie Antoinette lived at Fotheringay. Times were hard and the sisters and brother had to be resourceful to keep living in the house. Older citizens of the area remember going up to Fotheringay to have Annie tell their fortunes or to paying thirty-five cents for a tour of the house.

In 1952, the current owners' parents, Robert and Sarah Nutt, inherited the house and restored it to its original glory. Today, the house is enjoyed by the Nutts' grandchildren and great-grandchildren. "My kids spent summers at Fotheringay riding horses and ponies," says Julie Nutt Dalton.

Still a working farm, poled Herefords are raised on the 900 acres surrounding the house, and peaches and apples are grown in the orchard. "I love the house," says Julie Nutt Dalton. "It always feels friendly."

Unlike England's Fotheringay, visitors to this Fotheringay are delighted to stay—but are always free to go. ✒

Left: The circa 1820 dining table is original to the house and is set with the Dalton family's ironstone.

Hampstead

Above: The flying staircase ascends four stories, from the English basement to the third floor.

Hampstead's strikingly tall neo-classical exterior is but the beginning of the delights held in this Federal showpiece, built in 1820 by Conrade Webb. Historians believe that Webb, while a student at Brown University in Providence, Rhode Island, during the late 1790s, became familiar with the designs of New England architects Asher Benjamin and John Holden Greene. Indeed, much of Hampstead's detail appears to have been taken from Benjamin's book *American Builder's Companion* (1806), and the observation platform on Hampstead's roof is reminiscent of those designed by Greene for elegant city homes in Providence.

These influences may account for some of the features that make Hampstead truly unique, but current owners William J. and Phoebe Wallace say there remains a great deal of mystery about Hampstead's beautiful architecture. This mystery is part of the appeal of this great home, a mystery no doubt appreciated and added to by its succession of owners since Webb's death in 1842, when the

house and his estate were left to Webb's son Henry, who, in turn, left the house to his son Gordon Webb, who sold it in 1889 to J.L. Slaughter.

The decorative architectural details of Hampstead must have appealed to William Wallace's father when he bought the house in 1903. A Richmond architect, the senior Wallace purchased Hampstead at a time when the house had been greatly neglected. Sheep had been living in the basement, local farmers had stored grain on the second floor, and the family cemetery was a pigpen when the painstaking restoration began.

Although restored, Hampstead is largely unchanged from Conrade Webb's original plan. The imposing front door of the 1820s Federal house opens into a wide hallway that runs from the front to rear of the house, and is divided in its middle by an arch. To the left of the front door, behind a three-arched screen of columns, is a breathtaking flying staircase that hangs completely free of the walls. The stairway starts in the basement and continues to curve upward for four flights.

To the right off the main hall is the front parlor. The back parlor is directly behind the main parlor and is entered through enormous double doors that divide the rooms. Across the hall at the back of the house is a large formal dining room. On the second floor, the staircase screen is made up of three arches with Corinthian columns. The ceilings in the downstairs hallway have intricate, decorative plaster roundels and the double parlor ceiling is paneled in low relief. These architectural details make Hampstead one of the most ornamented Federal structures in Virginia.

The greatest alteration made to Conrade Webb's Hampstead is in the English basement. Webb had his library here, along with a wine cellar and some storerooms. The kitchen was in a separate building from the main house during Webb's era. Today, the old kitchen is

Left: The family cemetery at Hampstead is obscured from the house by long-established trees.

Right: An English dining table is surrounded by chairs purchased in New York.

Overleaf left: The unusual staircase rises behind a three-arched screen.

Overleaf right: The column-shaped pedestals in the front hall were a gift from the owners' nephews.

Each November, the Princess Anne Hunt
convenes at Hampstead for a day
of fox hunting on the property.

a ruin with just the chimney standing, and the English basement has been restored for use as a kitchen, bedroom, and art studio.

Hampstead has a commanding view of the Pamunkey River, which runs some distance below the house. The gardens to the side of the house are bordered by a curved brick wall. Large, old boxwoods line the walkway leading to the front door and enormous magnolias dot the front lawn. A county road runs along the north side of the property that reportedly was the route that Generals Washington and Rochambeau took to Yorktown to block British General Cornwallis. Today, the road leads past two brick gateposts which mark the entrance to Hampstead.

These views have inspired William J. Wallace all his life. A playground in his youth, the house is now a showplace for his and his wife's work. Both accomplished artists, the Wallaces' paintings hang on the walls of every room at Hampstead. Mr. Wallace built the beautiful, serpentine brick wall near the ruin of the old kitchen chimney. The wall serves as a backdrop for eye-catching perennial beds planted and maintained by Mrs. Wallace.

The Wallaces' children and grandchildren frequently visit Hampstead, as do hosts of other guests. The estate provides numerous opportunities for outdoor sports. Various local riders keep horses in the stable and each November the Princess Anne Hunt convenes at Hampstead for a day of fox hunting on the property.

Even though it had been sorely neglected, the beauty and distinctiveness of Hampstead has endured for 175 years. Both generations of Wallace men have appreciated the architectural uniqueness of the house and preserved it carefully. Conrade Webb's vision for his grand home, combined with Asher Benjamin's New England design influence, have made a lasting impression at Hampstead. ❧

Above: Riders from the Princess Anne Hunt gather on the front lawn.

Above right: The mantel in the former nursery is decorated with a Wallace sword.

Mount Ida

Above: The front parlor once served as a chapel for the Sisters of the Holy Cross, who occupied the house until 1992.

Like its namesake—the highest point on the island of Crete—Mount Ida is both a place of great beauty and an imposing presence on the landscape. Here, on a hill overlooking Alexandria, Mount Ida rises in the form of a neoclassical mansion, commanding a view of the Potomac River in the distance.

Mount Ida was once part of a 6,000-acre estate inherited by Charles Alexander, a sixth-generation descendant of John Alexander, for whom Alexandria is named. Alexander's original tract stretched two miles along the Potomac and encompassed what is now Arlington National Cemetery.

Mount Ida was, no doubt, a rural retreat in Alexander's time, but today it lies within the busy purview of metropolitan Washington, D.C. In 1805, when Alexander began construction of a four-room, two-story house on a hill that faced east toward the Potomac, the District of Columbia had been the national capital for only five years. Known in early documents as

"Charles of Mount Ida," Alexander was the beneficiary of land that had been part of an English patent purchased by his ancestors in 1669. The same year the federal government moved to the region from Philadelphia, Charles of Mount Ida married Mary Bowles Armistead, a daughter of a prominent Virginia family. When he died in 1812, Charles left Mount Ida and all the surrounding land to his oldest son, Charles Armistead Alexander.

By 1845, Charles Armistead's half-sister Eliza Selden owned Mount Ida. Eliza married John Janney Lloyd, and the house remained in the Lloyd family until 1907, when it was sold, along with 150 acres, to James Groves. In 1943, the mansion and the nine surrounding acres were purchased by the Congregation of the Sisters of the Holy Cross for use as a convent.

The Sisters converted the house's half dozen bedrooms into fifteen smaller bedrooms, and used the front parlor as their chapel. Mount Ida is located on the hill above St. Mary's Academy, where the sisters once served as teachers. Only three nuns remained at Mount Ida in November 1992, when Paul and Diane Mahefky purchased the house and undertook a major restoration, completing the work in 1993.

During the previous 180 years, Mount Ida underwent radical architectural changes. Previous residents had added rooms across the front of the house around the turn of this century, and the façade was made grander with the addition of Ionic columns and flanking porches. Inside the house, turn-of-the-century changes included arched doorways, an unusual stairwell and hall ceiling, and Beaux Arts panels and moldings throughout the first floor. In their renovation of the eleven-room structure, the

Above left: The elaborate doorway is reflected in the front hall mirror.

Above: Mount Ida offers a commanding view of the Potomac River to the east.

Overleaf: Mount Ida's stair seems to be missing its bottom portion (left). Actually, the first flight rises out of a side hall and joins the main stairwell on the second-floor landing (right).

Mount Ida was once part of a 6,000-acre estate inherited by Charles Alexander, a sixth-generation descendant of John Alexander, for whom Alexandria is named.

Mahefkys attempted to preserve the beauty of the interiors while making the house livable. They added French doors between many of the rooms on the first floor, replaced mantels and light fixtures, and used vibrant paint colors to augment the beautiful millwork and accentuate the high ceilings.

The interior layout of the house is complicated due to the changes and additions made to Mount Ida over the past two hundred years. The east-facing front door opens into a striking front hall, furnished with a Scottish tall-case clock and an antique English jockey scale that was once used to weigh in riders in the Derbies. The hall leads to a curious double stairway, the main part of which is enclosed between the dining room and the breakfast room to the west.

Beyond the front hall is the library, which dates from the original construction. The frieze and mantel there are both original, as is the adjacent breakfast room to the south. But the front portion of the house, consisting of the dining room, a parlor, and the entrance hall, were added by owners at the turn of the century.

The front parlor, located to the north of the entrance hall, is noteworthy not only for its view to the East, but also for its Federal-style antique sofa, needlepoint rug, and an antique English lectern.

"We were attracted to the house because of its style, particularly the columns in front," said Diane Mahefky. "Now I treasure its spaciousness. It's great for entertaining. We hold a cocktail party every year for our daughter's school. It's also great for just living. Really, Mount Ida is an ideal house for us in every way."

Left: The swags of fruit and flowers decorating the dining room mantel are motifs found in woodwork throughout the house.

Above right: The long front porch, protected by a tall hedge, offers guests a cool, shady place to relax.

Below right: The sun porch is a modern but welcome addition to Mount Ida.

Redlands

R edlands stands atop a broad knoll facing southwest toward Virginia's great Blue Ridge. Although not nearly as ancient as those mountains, the house is nevertheless an extraordinary testament to the longevity and persistence of Virginia's first families. Its current owners, the Carters, are the fifth generation of that family to have lived at Redlands since it was built around 1795. Their preservation of the home with its near-original features hasn't been an easy task.

In 1730, King George II granted the original Albemarle County tracts, some 9,350 acres, to John Carter, son of Robert "King" Carter (see Sabine Hall, page 102). The present mansion at Redlands was built in the late 1790s by John Carter's son Robert, around the time of the younger man's marriage to Mary Eliza Coles of nearby Enniscorthy. The house is one of seven extant estates located on the property comprising John Carter's original land grant.

Work on the residence at Redlands was not completed until the early 1800s. In 1809, Robert Carter died, leaving the plantation to his wife. In 1830, Mary Coles Carter divided the property among her four sons, leaving the residence and surrounding lands to her youngest son, Robert.

By the turn of this century, the Carters of Redlands were in dire straits. The house was owned by Robert Carter, an Episcopal priest who didn't have the wherewithal to keep up the grand old house. So his sisters, known in the family as Miss Sally and Miss Polly, decided to leave Redlands and go to Baltimore to found St. Timothy's, ultimately a very successful private school for girls. The hard-working Carter sisters are credited with keeping Redlands in the family and preserving an architectural gem, owned today by the

Right: The large front porch at Redlands offers views of the gardens and the Blue Ridge mountains beyond.

wife of another Robert Carter, the original owner's great-great-grandson.

Redlands is built both on and of the red clay soil that predominates southern Albemarle County, which gave the plantation its name. With a hipped roof and a distinctive modillion cornice, the well-proportioned Georgian structure is built of brick manufactured on the plantation. Its walls are laid in Flemish bond above the water table, and five-course American bond below.

The architecture of Redlands is unique in a number of ways. The front façade is Georgian, and the rear of the house is Federal. This architecture is reminiscent of Tidewater mansions built earlier, but historians consider the interiors at Redlands to be more sophisticated and innovative than those of its precursors. The front hall boasts an elliptical back wall, swagged arch, and hidden stairs. Like Jefferson at Monticello, the builder of Redlands chose to conceal the stairway behind a wall.

Directly behind the front hall is the large elliptical parlor, which features outstanding Adamesque woodwork. At the end of the room in the northern ellipse are three floor-to-ceiling, triple-hung windows, which function as doors to the outside. Unusually tall for the period, these windows give the room a French accent, another similarity to Monticello. The

Above far left: The Fitzhugh, Nanking, and Canton china at Redlands was brought to the United States on a clipper ship during the China Trade era.

Below far left: An upstairs bedroom provides ample sleeping space for a visiting family.

Above: The harpsichord was found in a chicken coop on the property.

Below left: The ceiling in the elliptical front hall gives the illusion of a swag.

159

The current owners are
the fifth generation of Carters
to inhabit Redlands since 1795.

Above: Sheraton chairs surround a wide mahogany dining table. Over the mantel is a painting of Robert Carter, who built Redlands nearly 200 years ago.

Right: Hanging on the walls between three triple-hung windows in the stunning elliptical parlor are a pair of French torcheres. To the left are a child's chair and a companion doll's chair.

proportions of the rooms are immense, especially in the downstairs rooms where the ceilings soar sixteen-and-a-half feet above the floors. The house has twelve fireplaces, including one in the English basement. Today, the enormous family kitchen is located in the basement, and to serve guests in the dining room, Mrs. Carter uses the home's original dumbwaiter.

Mrs. Carter and her sons maintain family tradition by using the acreage at Redlands as a working farm. Mrs. Carter's late husband, Robert, experimented with growing grapes and producing wine at Redlands. However, he later found it more productive to sell grapes to other wineries. Grapes grown at Redlands today include Chardonnay, Sauvignon Blanc, Merlot, and Cabernet Sauvignon. The Carters also grow hay and board horses.

The Carters have an unsentimental approach toward keeping Redlands. Mrs. Carter says she would never want her three grown sons to put the welfare of the estate ahead of their careers and families. One gets the sense though, that like Miss Polly and Miss Sally, the current generation of Carters will find a way to keep Redlands in the family for generations to come.

Left: The view of the Blue Ridge to the southwest of the house is beautiful in every season.

Above: The third floor dormers are typical of Redland's distinct Federal style.

Antebellum 1830–1860

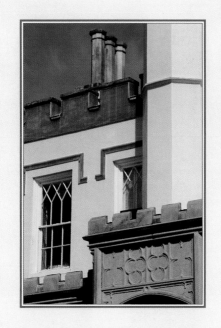

Welbourne

Welbourne stands imposingly behind a stone wall at the back of a sweeping, park-like lawn dotted with large old trees. Long side wings and tall white pillars give the house a classic southern colonial look. It is easy to imagine the hunt and hounds gathering in front of the house. In fact, Welbourne epitomizes the gracious, historic homes associated with northern Virginia's horse country.

Purchased by John P. Dulany in 1820, Welbourne has been the seat of seven generations of Dulany sportsmen and hunters. John's son, Richard Henry Dulany, founded the Piedmont Hunt in 1840 and the Upperville Colt and Horse Show in 1853, said to be the oldest horse show in the United States. John's father, Benjamin Tasker Dulany, was a Revolutionary War officer and fox hunting companion of George Washington.

The oldest part of the house dates from before the Revolution and now forms the main part of the south wing. John Dulany enlarged the house in 1820, when he added the two-story main section to the north. Sometime around 1830, one-story, octagonally-ended wings were added to the east and west of the main house. A two-story porch with slender, square columns was built across the front of the house in 1850, and the last structural change was made around 1870 with the addition of a two-story section on the rear of the south wing. All of these changes have given the house something of a T-shape.

The main entrance to Welbourne is at the base of the T. The wide center hall has an imposing arch at the rear, framing a view of the stair which rises perpendicularly to the main hall. To the west through the library is a guest bedroom and across the hall to the east is the parlor and the music room at the end of that wing. Behind the stair hall, in the oldest section of the house, is the dining room. Built-in open cupboards display some of the 200 pieces of the family's 1790s Limoges china.

The interior woodwork includes beautiful window surrounds with ornamented corner blocks and deeply molded mantel shelves supported by free-

Right: Sunlight and garden color flood the back hall at Welbourne.

It is not uncommon to have as weekend guests parents of nearby Foxcroft School students or foxhunters, who stay for days or even weeks.

Above: A guest room is made cozy by a four-poster bed and a fireplace.

Right: Cut-outs in the railings form elaborate shadows on the side and back porches.

Far right: A portrait of Colonel Richard Henry Dulany hangs in the parlor. Dulany led Virginia's 7th Cavalry in the Civil War.

standing columns that are typical of the region and period. Welbourne's three-part Greek Revival doorways that lead from the outside into the east and west wings add a distinctive architectural touch to the house. Behind the house are paths leading through enormous boxwoods and a covered porch on the east side of the house allows visitors to sit in the shade and admire the gardens below.

The house is currently occupied by a seventh-generation Dulany. Nathaniel and Sherry Morison inherited Welbourne from Nat's parents, Fanny Carter and Nathaniel Holmes Morison. Carrying on the family tradition begun by Nat's grandmother, Fanny Dulany Lemmon, they often fill the dining room and bedrooms at Welbourne with paying guests. Today, many of those visitors are parents of nearby Foxcroft School students or are foxhunters who stay for days or even weeks to enjoy the fine hunt country surrounding the estate.

Another tradition at Welbourne carried on by Nat and Sherry Morison is equestrianism. Horses have always been part of Welbourne's landscape. Notably, during the Civil War, Welbourne's owner Colonel Richard Henry Dulany led the Laurel Brigade, 7th Virginia Cavalry. While Dulany was

away in service, his prize stallion, Scrivington, was secreted away to Pennsylvania by his groom, where the horse was kept safe from Union seizure. Also, in 1905, Welbourne hosted the opening meet of the English-American Foxhound Match, and this, coupled with the plenitude of equestrian activity in surrounding Loudoun and Farquier Counties, led the area to be dubbed "the Leicestershire of America" in the early part of this century. Currently, seventy-five horses are boarded at Welbourne stables, and the Piedmont Hunt often begins its day of foxhunting on the front lawn of Welbourne.

Though Welbourne was the site of some raids during the Civil War—attested to by Mrs. Henry Grafton Dulany (Aunt Ida) of nearby Oakley in her journal entries of 1862 to 1863, in which she wrote "Welbourne has been stripped of everything"—its majesty has been preserved. The bookcases in the library are crowded with volumes of Civil War and Southern history, and portraits of family members who served in the Civil War illustrate the significance of the event in the family's history. The Morisons are extremely knowledgable of this history, and often recount it with pride as they lead guests on tours of the house and its many surviving outbuildings. Whether attending a Christmas party or staying as a paying guest for a weekend of foxhunting at Welbourne, everyone is invited to be an active part of this beautiful home's rich history. ❧

Above: Welbourne's woods provide wonderful places for its many boarders to ride their horses.

Right: Welbourne's aspect is that of the quintessential home for Southern gentry.

Brookview Farm

The house at Brookview Farm in Goochland County is seldom mentioned in the same breath as Virginia's grand old plantation homes—but what it lacks in grandeur it makes up for in charm. Once a part of Dover Plantation, the farm residence and its four nearest out-buildings were built in the 1840s as an overseer's house and slave quarters.

Despite their humble origins, these simple brick buildings have far outlasted the other elements of the plantation. Not only that, during the past decade, they have been lovingly transformed by the hands of Alexander M. Fisher, Jr., and his wife, Mary Ross, into a remarkably comfortable and interesting place to live. Sandy and Rossie Fisher have made a silk purse out of what some would have considered a sow's ear.

During the Civil War, Brookview Farm was an undifferentiated part of the bustling plantation owned by James D. Morson. The overseer's residence was located less than a quarter mile west of the main house and not far from an antebellum steam-powered mill. Morson's wife, Ellen, was sister-in-law of Confederate Secretary of War James A. Seddon, who lived on neighboring Sabot Hill Plantation.

The troops of Union Colonel Ulric Dahlgren raided both Dover and Sabot Hill during March 1864. On his way east to Richmond, where he hoped to free 12,000 Union prisoners, Dahlgren came to the two plantations after nightfall.

Morson was away on business that night and Seddon was off tending to the waning Confederacy. Confused about which house belonged to Seddon, Dahlgren attacked both houses, but was particularly aggressive in his vandalism of Dover, where his troops burned a stone barn and three stables with the horses still in

Above right: Once an overseer's cottage, the house at Brookview Farm is now the primary residence on a 600-acre working farm.

Below right: The antique dining table folds in half to make it more portable.

them. They set fire to the main house three times, but family and servants managed to extinguish the flames. The overseer's house and slave quarters were not damaged, presumably ignored because of their relative lack of importance. The mill also was burned, but its ruins remain and parts of it have periodically been excavated by archaeologists. Although it survived Dahlgren's seige, the main house at Dover was ultimately destroyed by fire in the early twentieth century.

Brookview Farm became a separate tract sometime after the Civil War, its latest incarnation just one of many the place has undergone during its 150-year history. Originally just two rooms, the overseer's house has grown larger by fits and starts. Near the end of the century, the owners added a second floor. A one-story addition was made to the rear of the house at the turn of the century, and still later, the owners built a second floor and outside stairs onto that addition.

All of these additions created the T-shaped house the Fishers purchased along with more than 600 acres of rolling Piedmont pastureland in 1981. By then, the interior had all been painted dark green and the windows were covered with artificial snow sprayed from an aerosol can, Rossie says.

Yet, the Fishers were confident that underneath it all was a charming house waiting to be restored. They painted the interiors white, installed eleven new windows, and in the living room, added an old heart pine mantel they had salvaged from another house. In 1987, they enlarged again with an addition on each corner of the rear of the house.

The oldest part of the house remains largely unchanged. A steep staircase just inside the front door divides the living room on the east from the library to the west. Above these two rooms are two large

Left: The back porch serves as a mud room for an active farm family.

Above right: Brookview Farm's original four slave quarters are still standing, including the one in the foreground that has been converted into the modern farm's office.

Below right: This collection of blue Edgeworth Tobacco tins has special meaning to Rossie Fisher, whose family owned the company.

The farm residence and its four nearest outbuildings were built in the 1840s as an overseer's house and slave quarters.

bedrooms with fireplaces. The turn-of-the-century addition contains a large informal kitchen where the family gathers around a soapstone woodstove. Upstairs in this section are two more bedrooms. The dining room is located in the new northwest wing and the southeast wing is a recreation room. Upstairs, the Fishers added an open sleeping porch.

The Fishers also have been restoring the four slave quarters, one of which they now use as an office for their working cattle farm. Sandy maintains a herd of 250 to 300 head, which he raises using a combination of modern and traditional methods. He uses no antibiotics or steroids for his animals, and also grows wheat, barley, corn, soybeans, and hay organically—using no chemical pesticides, herbicides, or fertilizers.

The Fishers find farm life comfortable. Rossie Fisher grew up at nearby Sabot Hill Farm. She and Sandy were cattle ranchers in Colombia for a number of years before returning to Virginia along with a notable collection of native art and artifacts that they have used to decorate Brookview Farm. The Fishers' two children, Jane and Murray, have grown up riding horses, fishing, and working on the farm.

"Living on a farm makes you much more in tune with the seasons," Rossie says. "Murray can build or fix anything. Jane loves animals and isn't afraid to work with big ones. There is a place for meaningful work in the country. That isn't something we'd experience elsewhere."

When they can take a break from farm work, the Fishers hitch their two black Percherons to their antique carriage, a Brewster wagonette brake, and go for a ride.

"This old house has a lot of distinction and charm," says Rossie. "It is always evolving, always changing. The old wood, the creaks and groans—it gives us a sense of continuity."

Left: The heart pine mantel in the living room came from another old house in Virginia. Above the mantel is a wall hanging the Fishers purchased when they lived in South America.

Right: An antique high chair and a handmade stool are kept near the soapstone woodstove in the kitchen.

Camden

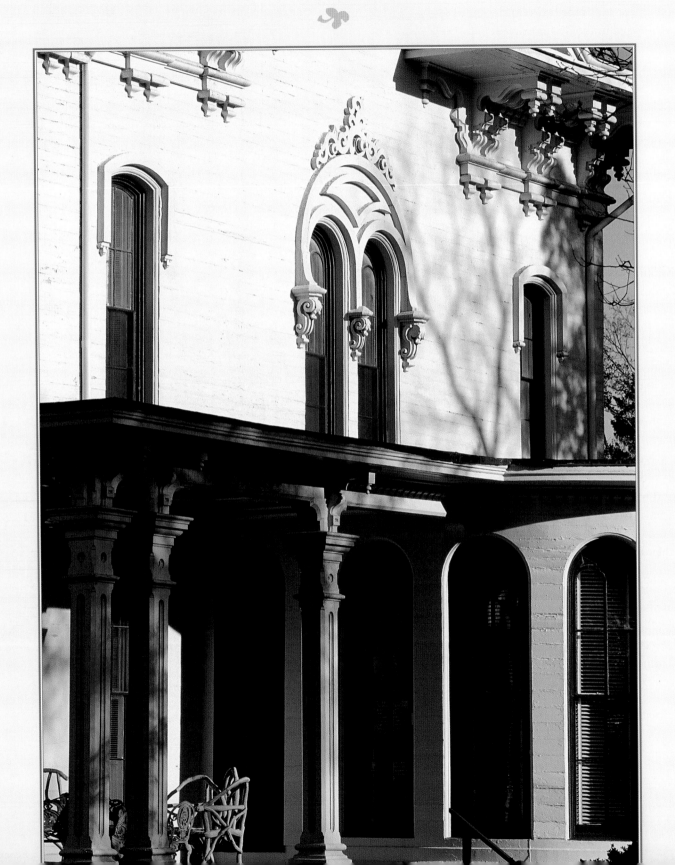

Three weeks before the Christmas of 1862, Union gunboats sailed up the Rappahannock River to a plantation near the town of Port Royal. On the south bank of the river, the plantation known as Camden was identified by an imposing mansion with a Tuscan-style tower. The captain of the gunboat Freeborn approached the house and spoke with young Eliza Pratt, the mistress of the house, as her husband, William Carter Pratt, was away at war fighting for the Confederacy.

The Union captain promised Mrs. Pratt that no harm would be done to Camden and rowed back to his gunboat. Yet within minutes, the boat's guns opened fire on the house. The first shell passed near Eliza's head as she leaned over her sick child's cradle in the downstairs nursery. In all, seven shells blasted through the house, destroying the tower and damaging the wood- and plasterwork. Today, the splintered holes in the second floor woodwork are testament to what happened that Advent season in 1862.

William Pratt had built Camden just three years prior to the Union attack as a home for his bride, Eliza, a Turner from the prominent planter family across the river. She had promised to marry William on the condition that he tear down the Pratt family's colonial-era house and build her something a bit more modern.

With the help of architect Norris Starkweather, Pratt erected a large, rambling house in the Italianate villa style so popular in the mid-nineteenth century. Yet Camden was unique in many ways. Cypress boards were used to cover the exterior. The boards were not overlapped, but

Above left: A portrait of the builder's father, John Pratt, hangs over the marble mantel in the dining room.

Below left: Arrowheads and other artifacts recovered on the property recall the Native American settlement that, as recently as 1608, populated the grounds at Camden, when John Smith sailed up the Rappahannock and created the first known map of the area.

butted flush. Sand was put into the paint that was sprayed (probably with a bellows) onto the boards to make the house look as though it was built of stone.

On the interior of Camden, Starkweather built in the latest inventions. Running water was available from silver spigots in every bedroom. The house boasted central heating, a cool air system, and gas lights.

Camden was built with a wide center hall that runs from the north (or river side) to the south (or land side) of the house. The beautiful curved staircase once led from the first floor up to the tower, which rose four stories before being shot off in the Civil War. On the west side of the house, Starkweather placed a one-story, curved room, with nine large windows, that was originally used as an orangery.

Today, the dirt floor of the orangery has been replaced with wood, but few other modifications have been made to the house since its construction in 1859. The parlor in the northwest corner of the downstairs is decorated with the original brocade drapes, Brussels carpets, and Belter furniture that Eliza Pratt ordered for her new house. White marble mantels brought by boat from Philadelphia and New York are in the downstairs rooms at Camden. The four main rooms were each designed with a different wood or faux wood trim. The parlor is rosewood, the library walnut, the dining room oak, and the main bedroom mahogany.

Above: Italianate architecture, popular in the mid 1800s, was elevated to elaborate heights in the design and construction of Camden.

Above left: The curved stairs once ascended to a tower room that was destroyed by shells shot from a gunboat during the Civil War.

Below left: The Rappahannock River flows past the front lawn.

Overleaf left: Original Belter furniture and a Brussels carpet still decorate the parlor.

Overleaf right: A view of one of many outbuildings on the property.

On the interior of Camden, Starkweather built-in the latest inventions. Running water was available from silver spigots in every bedroom.

Camden's current owner, Helen Pratt, is the daughter-in-law of Eliza Turner Pratt. Helen Pratt's late husband, Richard, spent most of his 102 years at Camden. Born in the big bed in the main bedroom downstairs in 1886, Richard Pratt died in that bed in 1988. Helen Pratt never knew her mother-in-law, Eliza, who died in 1928, but Richard Pratt made the family history about Eliza and the war come alive through his stories and recollections. Curiously, though, Richard would let no one record his stories. Today, Eliza Pratt's great-grandson, John Randolph Pratt, lives in a bungalow next door to the big house at Camden. Fortunately, he recalls many of his grandfather's wonderful stories and has compiled a notebook about Camden that includes the best of them.

Richard Pratt provided in his will for the preservation of Camden as a working farm and named John Pratt, his youngest grandson, manager of the farm. John manages the entire 500-acre estate, with 900 acres planted in feed corn, wheat, soybeans, and barley, and 600 acres left as natural woods and wetlands. The combination of open fields and woodlands provides for excellent hunting. Members of the Camden Hunt Club pursue deer, turkey, ducks, geese, and dove at regularly scheduled hunts. Stocked ponds on the farm offer fisherman bass and bream.

The first John Pratt arrived in Virginia in 1690 at Leedstown, across the river from Camden, beginning a legacy of more than 300 years of Pratts along the Rappahannock River. The current generation of Pratts have a strong sense of their past, not to mention a profound love for Camden. ✦

Left: An elaborately carved gilt mirror was the last purchase Eliza Pratt made for Camden before the Civil War.

Right: The carved door surround, intricate arches, and the curved staircase are typical Italianate touches in Camden's interior.

Glen Valley

Above: In the library, Tom May and Ben Armistead pay homage to England with a lithograph of Queen Victoria on the far wall, Royal Doulton plates and Staffordshire dogs on the mantel, and other British memorabilia placed artfully throughout the room.

Glen Valley—a three-story, gray farmhouse with its Greek Revival front gable—embodies the classic mid-nineteenth-century American country home, except that it is nestled into the slope of a hill instead of commanding its crest. Its location is perhaps to better afford a view of the Blue Run River, which flows across the back lawn on its way to the nearby Rapidan.

Dr. George S. Newman, an Orange County physician and farmer, built Glen Valley as his home. In the spring of 1853, Dr. Newman was employed as the surveyor of Gordonsville and laid out much of that nearby town as well. Orange County—formed in 1734 from land carved away from neighboring Spotsylvania County (named for Governor Spotswood, who had made the first passage across the mountains of Blue Ridge in 1716 on the Expedition of the Knights of the Horseshoe)—enjoyed a heyday in the 1840s and 1850s, and the nearby hamlet of Gordonsville had exploded into a transportation hub when two railroads and two east-west toll roads across the Blue Ridge converged in the county around the same time.

In 1855, at the peak of the Orange County-Gordonsville boom, Dr. Newman built Glen Valley, a five-room farmhouse with an English basement. Originally a side-hall house, Glen Valley had two large rooms to the east of the hall. These rooms now serve as a parlor/music room and the dining room. The kitchen, originally in the English basement, is now located in the newly-built west wing, along with a great room and two upstairs bedrooms. Because the house was built into the side of a hill, the English basement opens out onto ground level at the back.

The curved walnut staircase and railing in the front hall show that, while a farmhouse, Glen Valley was built with love and was intended to last. Before buying the house in 1990, owners Tom May and Ben Armistead had visited Glen Valley many times. As good friends of the previous owners, the two had often enjoyed dinner and other occasions at Glen Valley. They've made few changes to the house beyond an addition to the west and the structural alterations necessary for comfortable living. The parlor and dining room mantels, as well as the heart pine flooring, are original to the house. The decor, including English lithographs, Virginia antiques, and family pieces, fit comfortably into this nineteenth-century gem.

Gracious hosts, May and Armistead think nothing of entertaining even as many as 100 friends for a buffet following the November hunt races at nearby Montpelier, former home of James and Dolley Madison. Christmastime finds Glen Valley filled with family and friends. Overnight guests have learned that if they want a warm bedroom, they have to haul their own wood up to their fireplaces.

Wood is not the only thing hauled at Glen Valley. In the six years they have lived in the house, May and Armistead have found themselves hauling rocks, mulch, shrubs, and even trees.

Left: The terraced fish pond and extensive garden areas add natural grace to the back lawn at Glen Valley.

189

The wooded hillside leading down to the front of the house has been walled with field stones the two found on the property. Under the shade of the trees, azaleas bloom on the front hill each spring. In June, day lilies enliven the borders along the lawn, and the backyard pond is yet another focal point of this timeless home.

May and Armistead love Glen Valley, but admit it is a work in progress. Next on their list of projects is replacement of the drapes in the music room. Their goal isn't to change Glen Valley. Rather, it is to improve ever so slightly upon this wonderful old house.

Above left: The original portion of this 1850s house was a four-room structure with an English basement.

Below left: Alex, a cocker spaniel, rests in his basket in front of an English hand-tooled brass wood box.

Above: The lush gardens at Glen Valley give Tom May plenty of plant material for his floral creations.

Right: The dining room chandelier, purchased in a junk shop, was refitted with new prisms. The English silver epergne was a gift from Tom May's godmother.

Staunton Hill

Charlotte County's Staunton Hill—with its octagonal crenellated towers and clustered octagonal chimney pots—is virtually impossible to confuse with any other house in Virginia. Built in 1848 by Charles Bruce, this imposing structure stands on a hill overlooking the Staunton River. Having survived the Civil War undamaged, it serves today as the home of Bruce's great-grandson, David Surtees Bruce, and is the centerpiece for an inviting rural conference center.

Staunton Hill is Gothic Revival with a twist. When architect John Evans Johnson designed the house for Charles Bruce, he incorporated many classic Gothic Revival elements, such as pointed arches, clustered colonettes, and corner towers. In other ways, though, the house is decidedly un-Gothic, with its symmetrical and balanced façade and its stucco exterior, both of which give Staunton Hill more of an English Regency look.

Bruce apparently had the liberty to play around a bit. He was the son of James Bruce, said to be the third wealthiest man in early nineteenth century America, who had made his fortune growing tobacco and as a pioneer of chain-store retailing. And Charles Bruce was rather successful himself. Records show that he produced as many as 5,000 barrels of corn and a million hills of tobacco

Left: A close look at the double parlor reveals treasures from Italy, India, and China, as well as English and American furnishings.

193

annually on the 5,000 acres he had inherited from his father. So he spared no expense on the construction of Staunton Hill.

His architect, Johnson, used octagonals both outside and inside the house. The entrance hall is eight-sided, with a vaulted ceiling and statues of goddesses in niches around the perimeter. The marble for the floor in the hall and the marble mantels throughout the four main rooms downstairs was shipped from Italy to North Carolina, then brought by barge up the Roanoke and Staunton rivers to the site of Staunton Hill. Because of Staunton Hill's remoteness, in fact, most of the materials came by water.

The stair hall behind the octagonal front hall is impressive with its divided, curving stairs. These stairs draw the eye to the center of the rear wall, where a door leads to a study. Along the west side downstairs is a large parlor that may be divided into three areas by closing twelve-foot pocket doors. The eastern section downstairs holds a large dining room, a restaurant-style kitchen, and a breakfast room. Wood and plasterwork in the dining room dates from the 1930s, but other downstairs rooms retain original Gothic Revival cornices, woodwork, mantels, and gilt pier mirrors.

Staunton Hill's distinctive interiors provided a backup for Charles Bruce's noncombative involvement in the Civil War. A Virginia state senator from 1855 to 1863, Bruce hosted a meeting of the Confederate cabinet at Staunton Hill in 1865. His wife, Sarah Seddon Bruce, was the sister of James A. Seddon, the Confederate Secretary of War. Despite Bruce's connections with the Confederacy, no battles took place near Staunton Hill, and thus the house suffered

Left: Crenelated rooflines and leaded glass windows typify Staunton Hill's Gothic Revival style.

Right: The octagonal front hall boasts an Italian marble floor and statues of Venus, Bacchus, and Hermes.

none of the wartime destruction common among Virginia's antebellum homes.

When Charles Bruce died in 1896, none of his ten children chose to follow the rural lifestyle, and the Bruces briefly lost ownership of the estate. One son, U.S. Senator William Cabell Bruce of Maryland, spent weekends at Staunton Hill, but by the end of the 1920s, the house was being used as a hunting club. Then in 1933, the Senator's son, David K. E. Bruce, brought Staunton Hill back into the family.

This grandson of the original owner began making improvements immediately. Among his most notable additions were two one-story guest wings at the rear of the house and a portico, all designed by William Adams Delano. However, soon after completing these improvements, Bruce was called to London to head OSS operations in Europe, the first of a series of appointments in the foreign service, where he later served as Undersecretary of State and ambassador to France, Germany, England, NATO, and China. Although abroad much of the time, Bruce and his

Above: Long porches line both sides of the back courtyard.

Right: A brass deer that once belonged to Coco Chanel sits atop the stair hall table.

With its symmetrical and balanced façade
and its stucco exterior, both of which
give Staunton Hill more of an
English Regency look, Staunton Hill
is Gothic Revival with a twist.

wife, Evangeline, when in the United States, entertained prominent people at Staunton Hill, including Lady Astor and Secretary of State Dean Acheson.

Upon his retirement in the 1970s, David K. E. Bruce retired to Staunton Hill, then bequeathed the estate to his three children. Today, his eldest son, David Surtees Bruce, lives at Staunton Hill and, since 1984, has operated the estate as a conference center. This great grandson of the founder of Staunton Hill lived for many years in the Far East and traveled the world, returning to his ancestral home with artistic treasures he has used to decorate the home-cum-center.

Near the main house is a five-room Gothic Revival lodge that once served as the office for the plantation. Guests at the conference center may stay in rooms at the lodge or in the wings of the main house. The house and its wings form three sides of an enormous courtyard. Elsewhere around the house are gardens, a pool and pool house, several cottages, and the modern conference facilities.

The grounds at Staunton Hill are surrounded by an exceptionally wide, two-mile-long brick wall. Bruce urges his guests to use the wall as an elevated path for walking around the property—a decidedly un-Gothic way to view this one-of-a-kind Gothic Revival masterpiece. ❧

Left: Crenelated moldings mimicking Staunton Hill's Gothic Revival exterior top the original built-in bookcases in the library.

Right: The brick end of the west wing provides a sturdy backdrop for the rose garden.

Westend

Above: The lacquered, silk-inlaid card table is set for a game in Westend's little parlor. The portrait over the mantel is of Henry Taylor, the current owner's father.

Susan Dabney Morris Watson knew what she wanted—a house to call her own. In 1849, when Westend was completed, she had achieved her goal. Westend is a mansion of classical proportions, with Tuscan columns and brickwork painted to resemble stucco. Susan Watson was certainly acquainted with classical architecture and Jeffersonian tradition when she commissioned Colonel James Magruder to begin its construction in 1847.

Susan Dabney Morris and James Watson were first cousins who had grown up on neighboring plantations in the Green Springs section of Louisa County. Green Springs was a unique agricultural phenomenon in this area of the Virginia Piedmont when the Morris and Watson families (see Bracketts, page 118) settled it in the late eighteenth and early

nineteenth centuries. A 14,000-acre bowl of gentle hills and rich soil, Green Springs was first established for its medicinal springs and later for its fifteen-inch thick, fertile, gray topsoil.

After the death of her husband, Susan Watson, due to the paternalistic laws of the time, had to sue her husband's estate in 1837 to establish guardianship over her two children and to obtain her dower rights to the land her husband had left upon his death. She won her case and received 372 acres as her dower third one hundred along with the right to sell an additional 100 acres for the support of her children.

The Watson and Morris families were among many who built fine homes in the area, among them Ionia, Green Springs, Sylvania, Hawkwood, Grassdale, Kenmuir, Prospect Hill, Oakley, and Bracketts. By the late 1840s, when Susan Morris Watson was building Westend, Green Springs had become a thriving community with its own churches and even an inn. Westend was built at a cost of approximately $6,000, not including the cost of food and lodging for the craftsmen who worked on the house. While this sum may seem paltry now, Mrs. Watson's expenditures made it one of the grandest houses in the Green Springs neighborhood.

Susan Morris Watson's investment was a wise one, affording six generations of her family a luxurious home. In 1856, Mrs. Watson drew up an agreement with her son David Watson, her daughter Mary Minor Taylor, and her son-in-law Henry Taylor II that gave all but twelve acres and the house to her children. David Watson was killed at the Battle of Spotsylvania in 1864 and Susan Morris Watson died in 1869, leaving Mary and Henry Taylor 1,200 acres and Westend. Mary and Henry's unmarried daughters, Lucy and Mary, stayed on at Westend until 1960, when Lucy died. Lucy and Mary's nephew, Henry Taylor IV, took over the management of Westend in the 1950s, and

Left: The main hall is divided into a front reception area and a back stair hall.

Right: A framed piece of a "tumbling blocks" quilt that hangs on the wall of the transverse hall was left unfinished by maiden aunts who lived at Westend after the Civil War.

Susan Morris Watson built Westend at a cost of approximately $6,000, not including cost of food and lodging for the craftsmen who worked on the house.

Above: Much of the backing of this old quilt piece consists of old receipts and correspondence.

Right: Austere and elegant describe this upstairs guestroom, furnished with, among other pieces, an antique cradle and a handmade quilt.

today, his son Henry Taylor V and his wife, Ann, live at Westend.

From a distance, Westend looks like a Greek temple, set on a rise and supported by enormous columns. Closer inspection reveals a two-story center block house with two one-story wings with hipped roofs. Each wing originally contained an orangery on the south side. Today, the east orangery remains, but around 1900, the west orangery was converted into a bedroom and a bay window was added.

The central part of the house follows a conventional Virginia plan, with four rooms on each of the first and second floors radiating off a central hall. The central hall is comprised of two parts—an entrance hall in the front and a stair hall in the back. These two halls are divided by a louvered door set in a partition wall decorated with glass sidelights. The hall and all of the public rooms on the first floor have floor length, triple-hung windows that double as doors. To the east of the entrance hall is the front parlor, which opens to the back parlor through a set of pocket doors. Both rooms contain heavy, Roman-style cornice moldings.

To the left of the fireplace in the front parlor is a window that opens into the east orangery. The brick floor of this sunny room is some three feet lower than the parlor floor. Today, the back parlor serves as the formal dining room and is next to a large, modern kitchen set behind the east orangery. (The kitchens were originally located in two of four outbuildings behind the house that today include a farm office and storage buildings.)

To the west of the front hall is the library and in the west wing is a sitting room built in the former west orangery. Behind the sitting room in the northwest corner of the house is the master bedroom where the dining room was originally located. Guests could enter the dining room through a transverse hall that opened into the back hall at the foot of the stairs.

Henry Taylor has accomplished a massive restoration since he retired and moved to Westend two years ago. Formerly a contractor, Taylor had the desire and experience necessary to make Westend the grand home it once was. Taylor's first project required him to jack up the house and repair the foundations. That task was followed by six months of plaster work and the replacement of wiring and plumbing. He then redecorated, adding beautiful paint colors and Victorian wallpaper borders below the repaired and refinished cornice moldings. Family portraits, heirloom furniture, and antique silver seem right at home in this grand old house. His final project, as yet unfinished, is to restore the outbuildings and refurbish them for modern use.

Left: The original farm office at Westend, pictured in the foreground, sits adjacent to the old kitchen and slave quarters.

Woodside Farm

Most of Woodside Farm's history was unknown to owner Gay Estin the first time she visited the house, but the view from the front lawn of the nearby Cobbler Mountains convinced her to buy the place. After six years at this Fauquier County farm, Gay Estin is still learning the secrets of her house.

Originally a simple eighteenth-century, two-over-two-room house, Woodside was converted into a two-story Federal house with tall center chimneys around 1850. This nineteenth-century portion of the house was once covered with stucco on the front and sides, and the stucco and rear brick wall were painted white. Today, Woodside Farm's brick façade is simple and elegant, with little ornamentation or fuss. A stone terrace runs across the front of the house and the sloping front lawn is dotted with large poplar and linden trees.

Mirroring the exterior, the interior of Woodside Farm is understated in its simple elegance.

Above: A row of gleaming riding boots attests to Gay Estin's love of horses.

A wide center hall runs through the house in the wing built in the 1850s. To the east of the hall is a seventeen-foot by twenty-two-foot dining room with fourteen-foot ceilings and two tall, triple-hung windows. Across the hall to the west is the front parlor, with its large floor-to-ceiling bay window on the west wall. At the rear of the main hall are several steps leading down to the back hall, which connects the eighteenth- and nineteenth-century portions of the house. A staircase is on the west wall of the back hall and to the east is a large sunroom. At the rear of the house, in the older section, are a modern kitchen and family room, and upstairs, the two large front bedrooms are connected by a hall to the two bedrooms in the rear of the house.

Woodside Farm was once part of a large tract of land owned by Supreme Court Justice John Marshall. Upon the death of Marshall's son Thomas in 1831, the Justice's granddaughter, Anne Lewis Marshall, received Woodside Farm as her part of the family estate.

Anne had married John Fitzgerald Jones and they lived in the house until after the Civil War. Around 1880, Colonel Robert Beverley bought the house for his daughter Rebecca and her husband, Captain William Pinkney Herbert.

Three generations of Herberts lived at Woodside Farm until it was sold in 1983. The house then quickly changed owners a few times before Gay Estin bought it in 1990. After traveling for many years from her home in Aspen, Colorado, to Virginia for the hunt season, making do with a small log cabin as her hunt box, Estin decided to make Fauquier County her permanent home. Woodside Farm and the surrounding thirty-two acres allowed her to stable and care for her horses, while pursuing her interest in gardening as well.

Near an entrance on the west side of the house is Estin's herb garden, which is decorated with a millstone found on the farm. Her main perennial garden, now surrounded by a white board fence and espaliered apple trees, is behind the house in what was once just an open

Left: A German pewter chandelier hangs from the dining room ceiling, and a portrait of the owner and her brother hangs over the hunt board.

Right: An armoire found in Strasburg, Virginia, is a focal point in the austere back hall.

After six years at this Fauquier County farm, Gay Estin is still learning the secrets of her house.

Left: Two of Estin's many horses graze in front of the house.

Above: Hand-painted plates from Capri complement silver cups from India in Woodside Farm's dining room.

213

field with two old apple trees. Two outbuildings built of logs are located northeast of the house. One building was the smokehouse and the other may have been the original kitchen. Other outbuildings include the horse barn and assorted farm sheds.

An accomplished equestrian, Estin fox hunts regularly and is the co-owner of a local hunt concern which took first-place honors in the 1996 Middleburg Hunt Cup. She is also owner of a number of pieces of European decorative art. The house holds furniture from France, Italy, and Switzerland, all collected in Estin's travels, and Estin readily admits she has a particular love for things that are French. Her European pieces are successfully mixed with American antiques and furniture found in local shops.

Estin received some valuable advice from her good friend, the late Jacqueline Kennedy Onassis. "Jackie visited me often at Woodside Farm and loved this house," says Estin. "She encouraged me to learn the history of the house and to think of myself as the 'curator' of Woodside Farm."

Estin is still gathering historical details of Woodside Farm. She has learned, for example, that the marble fireplaces in the dining room and parlor are said to have come from the White House when it was remodeled around 1850. She also discovered that during some remodeling done by the Herberts, a wooden block was found in one of the walls.

On it is inscribed:

> James F. Jones married Anne L. Marshall,
> January 2, 1845. Their children Maria
> Cary R. Jones, Anne Lewis Jones, Thomas
> Marshall Jones, Fanny Barton Jones. This
> house was built by William S. Sutton
> carpenter, Luke Woodward brick mason,
> [illegible] plasterer, Leaky and Walker
> painters. 1851. June 1851—James F. Jones
> 30 years old, Anne L. Jones 29 years old,
> Cary 5, Nannie 4, Marshall 2, Fanny 9 months.

With this knowledge, Estin possesses quite an ample lead for further historical investigations of her beautiful Woodside Farm. ⚘

Left: A Renaissance painting by Sofonisba Anguissola hangs over the black marble mantel in the front parlor.

Above right: The fieldstone patio across the front of the house affords views of the Cobbler mountains in the distance.

Below right: The window bay in the parlor is filled with an eighteenth-century French settee found in Montreal.

This book was typeset in Garamond Regular with Caslon Open Face stand up caps.